THE FOREIGN POLICY PAPERS
Volume 1

4: The Yom Kippur War:
End of Illusion?

Harvey Sicherman

FOREIGN POLICY RESEARCH INSTITUTE
Philadelphia, Pennsylvania

SAGE PUBLICATIONS
Beverly Hills / London

For information address:

SAGE PUBLICATIONS, INC.
275 South Beverly Drive
Beverly Hills, California 90212

SAGE PUBLICATIONS LTD
St George's House / 44 Hatton Garden
London EC1N 8ER

International Standard Book Number 0-8039-0643-9

Library of Congress Catalog Card No. 75-44551

FIRST PRINTING

*When citing a Foreign Policy Paper, please use the proper form. Remember to cite
the series title and include the paper number. One of the two following formats
can be adapted (depending on the style manual used):*

(1) PFALTZGRAFF, R.L. Jr. and J.K. Davis (1975) "Japanese-American Relations in a Changing Security Environment." Foreign Policy Papers, I, 1. Beverly Hills and London: Sage Pub.

OR

(2) Pfaltzgraff, Robert L., Jr. and Jacquelyn K. Davis. 1975. *Japanese-American Relations in a Changing Security Environment.* Foreign Policy Papers, vol. 1, no. 1. Beverly Hills and London: Sage Publications.

CONTENTS

PREFACE

The true business of government, said Cardinal Richelieu, is to foresee problems and to administer appropriate remedies while time remains. This requires a combination of imagination, information and judgment rarely possessed by rulers. Equally rare, however, have been those occasions when all three were absent.

The twentieth-century contribution to foresight, particularly in international politics, has been technique. Spy satellites, computers and data banks supply vast and varied quantities of information, but man has been much less successful at contriving devices to stimulate the imagination. Nothing has been offered to improve judgment. Governments are still taxed by problems they did not anticipate, for which they possess no ready remedy; there is never enough time.

The October 1973 Middle East war epitomizes the twentieth-century political surprise. Information was surely not lacking. The Arab-Israeli conflict had already occasioned three wars in fewer than twenty-five years, and its virulence had hardly diminished with the passage of time. Furthermore, both the United States and Israel possessed ample evidence of the impending Arab attack well before the event. This did not save them from disastrous misjudgment.

Similarly, a great imagination was not required to foresee the oil embargo or the energy crisis. Such dangers had been discussed publicly and in transatlantic forums long before the war. But appropriate remedies were not taken in time, and when the embargo came the United States and her principal allies lacked both the machinery and the will to collaborate.

The surprise of the war indicated failures of judgment and imagination. To these must be added the magnitude of impact, which affects the anticipation of future problems. Indirectly, the October war influenced international economics through the oil embargo, which aggravated pricing trends, endangering prosperity and development in many countries. The conflict's effects on perceptions of international politics, however, may prove to have been even greater. It had become fashionable since the late 1960s to speak of a new international system where the growing interdependence of nations would be accompanied by greater cooperation among the stronger states, a disposition to settle disputes short of war, added emphasis on economic rather than military strength, and political relationships less inhibited by ideology. The events of October 1973 confirmed instead the benefits of traditional tactics in making war, withholding resources, threatening and deterring intervention. Interdependence was shown to be unevenly distributed; some were more "interdependent" than others, and cooperation was not necessarily the lesson to be learned.

The effect of the war on perceptions of the international system was especially important for the United States, which had taken the lead in extolling the potential of the new international "multipolarity." The Nixon administration elevated change to the status of a doctrine and consciously designed a foreign policy to accord with the "new realities." Washington proclaimed "new centers of power," a "new" relationship with the Soviet Union and a "new" opening to the People's Republic of China, hoping that a judicious combination of American strength, allied contributions and adversary negotiations would sustain vital interests despite reduced American commitments. The surprise and magnitude of the Yom Kippur War cast a dark shadow across such hopes, particularly those concerning the Soviet Union, the strength of U.S. allies and the American role itself. The war shook confidence in the accuracy of Washington's view of the world.

The effects of the Yom Kippur War, or the "War of the Day of Judgment," as the unlucky Israeli chief of staff called it, promise to influence international politics at least for the remainder of this decade. It is therefore vitally important to understand its causes, to chart its impact and to deal with its consequences. This paper seeks in particular to expose the illusions that distorted Israeli and American judgments before October 1973 and to illuminate the war's implications for the United States. Only by discarding such illusions and by understanding the implications of the war can the foundations for an effective U.S. foreign policy be laid.

1. PROLOGUE TO THE WAR

The "State of War"

The Arab-Israeli conflict embodies the major political passions of the twentieth century: the fears of minorities, nationalism, the clash between Western technology and traditional societies, the hopes and disappointments of industrial development. These passions are reflected in the positions of the main antagonists. The history of the Jews is replete with exile, suffering, dependence and disaster. Zionism's purpose was to ensure Jewish survival through territorial roots, self-government and secure national independence. Though never exiled and boasting a proud military tradition, the Arabs early lost control of their fate. Dominated by the Ottoman Turk for half a millenium and later by European empires, the Arabs were deeply humiliated by their subjugation. The ideologies of Arab nationalism advocated independence, Arab unity, Islamic renewal and the acquisition of modern technology as crucial to an Arab renaissance.[1]

Despite its great success in establishing the state of Israel, the Zionist movement offended both traditional Muslims and the new nationalists in the process. To the former, Zionism was an impious elevation of the protected but inferior Jew; to the latter, it was a grotesque neo-imperialism, designed to forestall Arab unity. In the quarter-century of her existence before the October 1973 war, Israel became an inseparable element in the "culture conflict" between Arab society and Western civilization, a convenient explanation for Arab failings as well as the major stimulus to Arab cooperation.[2]

On the surface, the Arab-Israeli dispute appears to be a grossly unequal contest. The Arab states are populous, possess valuable resources and occupy strategic territory. Israel is well placed and its population skilled, but the country lacks resources and the Jews are not numerous. In view of these facts, the Zionist leadership soon became convinced that Israel's survival depended on her willingness and ability to fight.[3] Arab advantages in numbers might be offset by an efficient military force with two goals: (1) rapid, total mobilization and (2) speedy victories, achieved by disruption of the opponent's offensive capacity rather than through direct annihilation. Total mobilization was Israel's only hope of obtaining temporary superiority of force; the indirect approach was the only way to avoid catastrophic casualties. Nonetheless, the major Arab assets, such as petroleum resources and transit routes, were presumed by the Israeli leaders to be so durable that the major international powers would not tolerate a complete Arab military debacle. This strategic "fact" could be mitigated only if Israel secured recognition by the great powers that while her survival threatened no one's vital interests, her disappearance would upset the balance among them. A lengthy, costly war waged in political isolation was believed to be simply beyond the strength of the Jewish state.[4]

Arab strategies were more complex because the struggle with Israel took place in the context of inter-Arab quarrels. Egypt, the largest and most powerful state, had developed separately from the other Arab national movements, and Egyptian fidelity to the Arab cause was constantly suspect as a blind for hegemony.[5] The Syrians, considering themselves to be the natural leaders of the Arab world, saw Palestine and Jordan as part of a greater Syria under Baathist ideology. The Hashimites in Jordan and Iraq had their own schemes for unifying their realms with Syria; after 1958, the surviving Hashimite in Jordan concentrated on survival. The new Baathist rulers in Iraq proved to be rivals of Syria. The conservative Wahhabi Muslims in Saudi Arabia and the petty sheiks and princelings of the Persian Gulf sought to preserve themselves against the "radicalism" of the Baath Party and Nasser through cash and Islamic sentiment. These quarrels and the irregular pace of political and economic development sustained the Arab world's reputation for instability and violence.

The "great powers" remained ambivalent about the Arab-Israeli dispute. Britain and France exercised historical influence in the Middle East with dominant interests in the Suez Canal, North Africa and the oil fields of Arabia and the Persian Gulf. But their attempts to retain authority, frequently by playing off local antagonists, did not succeed. The British position declined rapidly after the 1956 Suez debacle, and London announced the end of its commitments to the Persian Gulf sheikdoms in the late 1960s. During the fifties, the French had allied closely with Israel as part of their costly and vain attempt to keep Algeria, an alliance abandoned suddenly by Paris at the outbreak of the 1967 war. The United States, whose principal material interest consisted of American oil company concessions, supported Israel within a range of occasional pro-Arab posturing and attempts to enlist the major Arab states in anti-Soviet pacts as part of Cold War strategy. American reluctance to supply arms to Israel directly faded as the European states lost influence. In all the Western democracies, public opinion, stimulated in part by effective Zionist lobbies, largely favored Israel.

The Soviet Union pursued an equally complex course. Moscow supported the establishment of Israel in 1948 and helped her to survive with Czechoslovakian arms. Perhaps Stalin hoped that the Marxist-socialist wing of Zionism might triumph, giving the Soviets a friendly base in the then Western-dominated Middle East. In any event, the purges and anti-Jewish show trials of Stalin's last years soon soured the relationship.[6] Once Abdel Nasser of Egypt indicated his desire to break free of British influence and to oppose the American-inspired Baghdad Pact, Moscow initiated a heavy and sustained effort to associate Egyptian and Soviet objectives, offering both arms and economic assistance.[7] The Egyptian relationship would enable the U.S.S.R. to outflank the Baghdad Pact and to facilitate the expansion of Soviet influence throughout the Middle East.

Initial Egyptian efforts concentrated on Arab unity, Soviet military assistance and Western rivalries in order to assert Arab independence and threaten Israel. In 1956 Israel frustrated this strategy by attacking an Egyptian army that was accumulating Soviet armaments. The settlement of 1957 required a UN force and a partial American guarantee of free passage through the Strait of Tiran before Israel would withdraw from the Sinai. Ten years later, these arrangements proved no barrier to renewed warfare. After several spectacular fedayeen raids, sponsored by Damascus, Israel retaliated heavily. Egypt, her prestige seriously weakened by the misadventure in Yemen, concluded a mutual defense treaty with Syria. The Soviet Union, main arms supplier of both Egypt and Syria, encouraged Nasser to believe that Israel was about to attack Syria; in May 1967 he mobilized Egyptian forces and marched them into the Sinai.[8] A blockade of Israeli shipping was declared, and the other Arab states rallied to Egypt's lead. In response to Cairo's demand, the UN forces were promptly withdrawn. Meanwhile, the U.S. and West European governments temporized, astonished at the rapidity with which the crisis had developed.

Israel struck at this combination with her only strategy: complete mobilization and destruction of the enemy's offensive potential. The Israelis were fortunate that both Jordanian and Syrian offensive capability depended on Egyptian air support. After the destruction of the Egyptian Air Force during the first few hours of the war, on June 5, 1967, Israeli forces were able to rout the Arab armies in only six days; they captured the entire Sinai peninsula, half of Jordan and much of the Syrian Golan plateau. A Saudi-led oil embargo and an Egyptian blockade of the Suez Canal could not compel outside intervention against Israel.

Political Positions After the Six-Day War

The Six-Day War concluded a sequence of events that neither the local states nor the major powers had expected to culminate in conflict, and the old assumption about great-power interest in preventing a complete Arab disaster had not been entirely displaced by the rapidity of the victory. Her political and military prestige damaged, the Soviet Union apparently threatened intervention to prevent an Israeli attack on Damascus, a maneuver to which Washington responded with firmness toward Moscow and a cautionary note to Israel.[9] But Egypt and Syria were rearmed substantially during the summer of 1967 through a large air and sea operation that demonstrated Moscow's ability to intervene and sustained Arab resistance to negotiations with Israel.[10]

While the Soviet Union had the most to lose, other states were also disturbed by the war's outcome, and Israel's own diplomatic position was undercut by French and American actions. Israel's desire to retain some of the territories occupied during the war was not endorsed by her major political allies, even in the moment of victory. President de Gaulle's abrupt termination of the close Franco-Israeli relationship could be explained as an anti-American maneuver or as the posturing of a frustrated second-rate power. American plans for a Middle East settlement, prescribing complete Israeli withdrawal in return for *de facto* conclusion of Arab belligerency, could not be so explained.[11]

The occupied territory brought other problems for Israel. Conscious of Moscow's humiliation, Defense Minister Moshe Dayan thought Israel might do better by stopping short of the Suez Canal, thereby avoiding any direct clash with Soviet global interests in keeping it open.[12] There were even better military reasons. A canal position required long, vulnerable supply lines over difficult terrain, one of the major Egyptian disadvantages during the recent war. Furthermore, Israel had to maintain order in the West Bank and Gaza Strip, where considerable Arab populations had every stake in making the occupation difficult. Lastly, Israeli forces had been bred on a strategy of rapid thrusts into enemy territory. After 1967 offensive· action could only mean the invasion of Egyptian, Jordanian and Syrian heartlands, the occupation of their capitals and the overthrow of their governments. A defensive position meant restricted mobility, with large numbers of troops vulnerable to harassment designed to inflict maximum casualties—an acutely sensitive situation for the small, closely knit Israeli society.

The Arab states, especially Egypt, were also faced with a complete reconstruction of their strategy. Militarily shattered, demoralized and humiliated, the "front-line" governments— Egypt, Syria and Jordan—could not long remain inactive in the face of the Israeli occupation without endangering their own survival. Other Arab states, principally Saudi Arabia and the Gulf sheikdoms benefited immediately by Nasser's defeat, which concluded the Egyptian attempt to extend her "radical" influence to the Arabian peninsula. But these traditional regimes shared in the Arab humiliation and feared the spread of a different radicalism— that of the Palestinian guerrilla movements. In the war's aftermath, these guerrillas had attacked the Israeli conquerors in a defiant and popular compaign, albeit a political and military failure. In Kuwait and elsewhere, Palestinians were stirred by their exploits, and the guerrilla groups themselves espoused various revolutionary dogmas, some advocating the overthrow of Arab kings and sheiks as a prerequisite for the war against Israel.[13] The Saudi, Libyan and Kuwaiti governments soon supported both the front-line Arab states and the Palestinian organizations for ideological as well as practical reasons; in their view a persistent stalemate endangered their own stability.

The first joint Arab attempt to deal with the consequences of defeat took place at the August 1967 Khartoum summit. The meeting was dominated by a belligerent mood that drew strength from the Soviet arms supply and the war subsidies offered by Kuwait, Libya and Saudi Arabia. Eight Arab heads of state (Syria refused to participate, and Tunisia's Habib Bourguiba condemned the "belligerency policy" as a dead end) committed themselves to joint political and diplomatic action aimed at ensuring Israel's withdrawal "within the framework of the basic Arab commitment, which entails non-recognition of Israel, no conciliation nor negotiation with her and the upholding of the rights of the Palestinians to their land."[14] The Khartoum conference sank the initial U.S.-Soviet effort to create a Middle East settlement on the basis of plans acceptable to both sides—plans far-reaching in their assumptions of Israeli acquiescence, for they involved complete Israeli withdrawal in return for an end of the state of belligerency.[15] Israel's national unity government, formed in controversial circumstances on the eve of the war, was thus spared the difficulties of decision that an Arab agreement to the great-power plan might have presented.[16]

Efforts to devise a diplomatic solution were given further impetus on October 21, 1967, when Soviet Styx missiles sank the Israeli destroyer *Elath*; two days later, Israeli jets destroyed the oil refinery complex at Port Suez. On November 22, the UN Security Council, under the pressure of impending hostilities, adopted Resolution 242, which endorsed the main points of both sides—withdrawal, negotiations—while carefully leaving ambiguous the contradictory elements in both positions. Thus, Israeli forces should withdraw "from territories occupied in the recent conflict," not from *all* the territories. (Israel accepted the English version, not the French with the definite article.) The Arabs were not obligated to recognize Israel by name, but were required to terminate belligerency and acknowledge certain rights to exist for "every state in the area." The "refugee problem"— already an archaic formula in view of the Palestinian guerrilla groups—was to be settled "justly"; there was to be freedom of navigation through international (not defined) waterways. The "inadmissibility" of territorial acquisition by force and the need for peace and security for all area states were "emphasized." Finally, a special UN representative was designated to "assist efforts" at settlement; endorsement of direct or indirect negotiations was carefully avoided.

The "War of Attrition"

The UN Special representative, Swedish Ambassador to Moscow Gunnar Jarring, soon encountered the contradictions noted above as he attempted to facilitate talks. Israel stressed direct negotiations, peace treaties and territorial readjustment; Egypt and Jordan emphasized that Israel should commit herself publicly to complete withdrawal and that indirect negotiation should establish the "timetable" along with the political commitments to conclude the withdrawal. By the year's end, Jarring could not report progress toward bridging these positions.

The diplomatic option had thus been played out by the end of 1968. War soon resumed. Though on a different scale than the 1967 conflict, the "war of attrition" (1969-1970) was marked by increasing violence, expanding Soviet military intervention and extensive American diplomatic activity. Beginning in October 1968, the Egyptians bombarded Israeli canal positions, causing considerable casualties. Israel's retaliatory raids forced the evacuation of civilians from Ismailia and Port Suez, but she was restricted from choicer targets at Alexandria and Port Said by the presence of Soviet warships.[17]

The next step was taken by Israel in the construction of the "Bar-Lev line," fortified bunkers designed to protect Israeli forces against Soviet-supplied heavy artillery. On April 1, 1969, Nasser responded by announcing the abrogation of the cease-fire. Fresh Egyptian attacks along the length of the canal were accompanied by Palestinian incursions from Jordan, Syria and Lebanon intended to open a second front in the "occupied territories."

It was neither economically nor politically possible for Israel to sustain a very large standing army exposed to constant losses. Israel's counter to attrition was escalation, primarily through heavy air force bombardment of Egyptian lines. During January 1970, Israel used her newly acquired Phantom F-4s to extend her bombing campaign to Egypt's interior. These raids were intended to demoralize Egypt and perhaps topple Nasser.[18] More than 600,000 Egyptian civilians had to be evacuated, all the SAM defenses were lost and one-third of Egypt's front-line aircraft downed; but the artillery emplacements were too well fortified to be destroyed.

As hostilities expanded throughout 1969, the United States and the Soviet Union made another attempt to reach political agreement. The new Nixon administration, preoccupied with the Vietnam war, immediately conceded two major points to Moscow: first, the United States would engage in private talks with the U.S.S.R., without Britain and France (who were to be "informed" through the four-power talks), thus granting the Soviets a stronger "legitimacy" in any settlement; second, the talks would be aimed at "guiding" the local states, a position directly at variance with Israeli insistence on local negotiations without interference. Predictably, the powers were able to agree on a series of measures unacceptable to both Israel and the Arabs. A U.S. note (based on the Sisco-Dobrynin discussions) sent to Britain, France, Israel, Egypt and Jordan on October 28, 1969, was designed to establish a "guide" for a second Jarring mission to settle the Egyptian Israeli frontier. The note incorporated the "Rhodes formula" for negotiations (that is, under the aegis of a mediator), a three-month timetable for Israeli withdrawal after agreement on borders and refugee repatriation, and compensation according to agreed formulas.[19] The United States also designed a similar agreement for the Israeli-Jordanian frontier. These two formulations, later known as the Rogers Plan when they were publicly revealed in modified form by the American secretary of state in December 1969, also fell victim to the battlefield situation. They were rejected strenuously by all parties, especially Israel.[20]

The Egyptian answer to Israeli escalation with American aircraft was Soviet missiles, planes and pilots. After an emergency visit to Moscow from January 22 to 26, 1970, Nasser obtained Soviet assistance in defending the country's interior, but not long-range aircraft for retaliation against Israeli cities. The extent of the build-up surprised the United States and Israel. By mid-April more than 10,000 Soviet personnel were in Egypt, enjoying exclusive use of certain airfields and harbor facilities. In the face of Soviet intervention, Israel suspended the deep-penetration raids and concentrated on the front lines, inflicting more than 10,000 casualties during the spring offensive. Egypt renewed assaults on Israeli canal positions. American diplomacy seemed powerless to arrest the drift toward war or the expansion of

Soviet intervention. By May 1970 the Nixon administration, then conducting the Cambodian invasion, and committed to improving relations with the Soviet Union, launched a determined effort to "stop the fighting and start the talking." This was the Rogers peace initiative of June 1970, which was accompanied by strong intimations from the White House that Soviet intervention would be resisted. [21]

Both the Egyptian and Soviet governments saw in the Rogers initiative an opportunity to secure their objectives without trusting further to the fortunes of war or courting a confrontation. On July 22, 1970, Egypt accepted the proposal for a ninety-day cease-fire, a "standstill zone" and immediate resumption of negotiations. If the United States could be persuaded that a settlement favorable to Arab claims should be extracted from Israel, lest a new war with Soviet participation occur, then the war of attrition would accomplish its task.

Israel, which had resisted the Rogers proposal for fear that it would commit the government to the original Rogers Plan, was now isolated. A presidential message, Egyptian agreement and the inexorable movement of the SAM missile systems toward the Suez Canal convinced Premier Golda Meir (Levi Eshkol died on February 26, 1969) to accept the cease-fire line on July 31, 1970, even at the cost of reconstituting her national unity government on a more partisan basis when the Gahal opposition resigned in protest. [22] But in order to strengthen their threat, both Moscow and Cairo violated the terms of the cease-fire by moving missile installations forward to the canal's edge. [23] This shortsighted maneuver and Washington's belated recognition of the violations forced the United States to "rectify" the situation with a fresh arms supply for Israel, [24] thereby weakening American leverage in behalf of the Rogers Plan. Finally aroused by Soviet and Egyptian duplicity, the United States committed $500 million in arms shipments to Israel and demanded political "rectification" before further talks would be conducted.

While the cease-fire violations cost Egypt goodwill in Washington, the Arab "Eastern front" collapsed into the Jordanian civil war when the Palestinian irregulars failed to appreciate

Nasser's strategy and refused to abide by the cease-fire. King Hussein was endangered briefly by a Syrian tank invasion, abetted (in Washington's view) by Moscow. Surprisingly strong resistance by the Jordanians and ostentatious American-Israeli preparations to intervene brought about new restraint from Moscow and Damascus. [25] The Syrian forces withdrew, and the Syrian government was promptly overthrown by Air Force Commander Hafez al-Assad.

The loss of American leverage on Israel because of Washington's failure to rectify the cease-fire violations, the Jordanian civil war, Washington's alarm over Soviet behavior, and Nasser's death on September 28, 1970, exhausted the pressure produced by the war of attrition. During the remainder of 1970 and through most of 1971, the crisis atmosphere dissipated as peace efforts failed. After three years of stalemate, Gunnar Jarring, the UN special representative charged by Resolution 242 to facilitate a settlement, sought "parallel and simultaneous commitments" by Israel and the U.A.R. "which seem to be inevitable prerequisites of an eventual peace settlement between them." [26] These involved chiefly Israeli withdrawal to the 1967 prewar borders, with "practical security arrangements" for Sharm el Sheik, demilitarized zones and free passage through the Suez Canal. The U.A.R. would enter a peace agreement, including recognition, termination of belligerency and control of hostile acts (such as Palestinian raids). Significantly, Jarring's request for "prior commitments" was subject to the "eventual satisfactory determination of all other aspects of peace settlement, including in particular a just settlement of the refugee problem."

The Egyptian government, headed by one of Nasser's old revolutionary friends, Anwar es-Sadat, saw an opportunity to break free of the Khartoum resolution without yielding its basic negotiating position. By answering Jarring in the "qualified affirmative," Sadat became the first Arab leader to speak officially of a possible peace treaty with Israel, while reserving the details for his own later interpretation. [27]

The Israeli government, headed by Golda Meir, proved much more hostile to the Jarring initiative. It viewed the UN mediator's activities as an attempt to avoid direct Arab-Israeli negotiations and as a rhetorical trap, compelling Israeli commitment to complete withdrawal without clear and binding statements from Egypt. On February 26, 1971, the Israeli ambassador to the UN, Yosef Tekoah, conveyed to Ambassador Jarring a message addressed to the Egyptian government that "Israel will not withdraw to the pre-June 5, 1967 lines." Displaying extreme contempt for the UN and for public images, the Meir government restated Israel's unwillingness to accept third-party mediation or full withdrawal. The Jarring mission had come to an end.

Israel's stubborn rejection of the Jarring mission proved costly. During May 1971 the so-called Davignon Commission, the first effort by the European Economic Community to devise a common foreign policy, was prepared to recommend yet another Jarring mission on the basis of an eventual total Israeli withdrawal; the West German government blocked the effort after Israeli protest. A committee appointed by the Organization of African Unity also failed to restart the Jarring effort; though Israel this time behaved in a more conciliatory manner, the Africans were dismayed by Jerusalem's approach.[28] The United States also sought to convince Israel of the soundness of exchanging territory for international guarantees as the prerequisite for restarting the negotiating process. This led in March 1971 to the most acrimonious American-Israeli exchanges. At one stage, Secretary.William Rogers' international guarantees turned out to mean American willingness to participate in a mixed great-power force responsible to the UN Security Council, an arrangement regarded skeptically by both the Israeli government and the U.S. Congress. The Rogers effort foundered in April, a victim of the declining prestige of the UN, the Israeli experiences of 1967 and 1970, and popular American antagonism toward new military commitments in the wake of the Vietnam war.

During May 1971, Washington sought to extricate its peace initiatives from these complications through the so-called interim agreement to reopen the Suez canal. Such an agreement might be the first step toward a broader settlement. While the Soviet Navy would benefit the most from the canal's reopening, the Suez battle line, with its overtures of American-Soviet confrontation could be eliminated.

The U.S. proposals were thus designed to suggest more than simply the reopening of the canal, while reassuring Israel that nothing would be bargained away in advance. [29] But the Egyptians insisted on a military presence in the Sinai—or the right to one—as part of the deal. Again the discussion of guarantees for Israel in such a scheme eventually surfaced in the notion of a UN four-power force in the Sinai, but Israel had fundamental objections to such a proposal. Turning to more personal statesmanship, Secretary Rogers and Assistant Secretary Joseph Sisco toured the Middle East in May to promote their "good offices"; they returned with their good offices under considerable suspicion. [30] When Secretary Rogers offered the interim agreement to the UN General Assembly in October 1971, it was already a futile gesture. [31]

Détente and the Middle East

Since 1967 major American diplomatic initiatives—the great-power talks, the December 1969 Rogers Plan, the peace initiative of June-August 1970, the "international guarantees" argument and the interim agreement to reopen the Suez Canal—had foundered on the same problems:

(1) refusal of the Arabs and Israelis to agree on an interpretation of Resolution 242,

(2) Moscow's fluctuating diplomatic position and persistent military intervention, and

(3) inability to convince Israel that full withdrawal to the June 5, 1967, lines would assure Israel's security in the context of Arab political concessions and international guarantees.

During this period, the Soviet and American diplomatic positions were much closer to one another than to those of their respective clients. Nonetheless, Moscow and Washington were either unwilling or unable to synchronize the movement of their political positions with local military activity, stimulating in the process strong suspicions of insincerity.[32] But the August 1970 cease-fire had remained intact, reducing the chances for American-Soviet confrontation.

In Washington's view, the cease-fire violations were part of a larger pattern of increasingly ambiguous Soviet behavior. On September 16, 1970, at the height of the Jordanian crisis, with Soviet activity at the Cuban naval base Cienfuegos also alarming him, Dr. Kissinger told reporters:

> Our relations with the Soviet Union have reached the point where some important decisions have to be made, especially in Moscow. . . . Events in the Middle East and in other parts of the world have raised questions . . . specifically, whether the Soviet leaders are prepared to forego tactical advantages they can derive from certain situations for the sake of the larger interest of peace.[33]

The issues of "tactical advantages" and "larger interests," crucial to the development of Soviet-American détente, had grown more acute during the fall of 1971, as the United States prepared to initiate a new relationship with the People's Republic of China. The Indo-Pakistani war of November-December 1971 suggested a dangerous pattern: a Soviet-armed client dismembered an opponent considered important to regional stability by both Washington and Peking, neither of which could save the Pakistanis from defeat. The parallel with the Middle East seemed striking, especially because the Soviet Union and India had concluded a treaty of friendship in August remarkably similar to the Soviet-Egyptian treaty of May 27, 1971. Reviewing these events, President Nixon concluded that

> Soviet policy, I regret to say, seemed to show the same tendency we have witnessed before in the 1967 Middle East war and the 1970 Jordanian crisis—to allow events to boil up toward crisis in the hope of political gain.[34]

Nonetheless, the United States did not intend to abandon her pursuit of better relations with the Soviet Union; indeed, the president's new opening to Peking, the Vietnam negotiations,

SALT I and the September 1971 Berlin Agreement were all evidence of Washington's assumption that Moscow could be brought around to more restrained and stable behavior. The two levels of U.S.-Soviet exchange—the strategic and the regional—remained to be coordinated or "linked." As Nixon reportedly said to Brezhnev on May 24, 1972, during the Moscow summit, "if the Soviet Union's allies attack America's allies with Soviet equipment, the United States has no choice but to react."[35] In other words, the progress of strategic compromise and agreement would not hamper an American response to attempted Soviet exploitation of regional difficulties. The necessity for such re-action and its frequency would inevitably affect the general tenor of the Soviet-American dialogue, although the point of impact remained ambiguous. It was this assured response and its poten-tial impact on détente, rather than any conviction on Nixon's part about Soviet intentions, that constituted the ultimate strength of "linkage."

Public evidence that such a linkage was being drawn between the Middle East and détente appeared in the president's State of the World message to Congress on February 9, 1972. Criticizing the Soviet role in the region over the past five years, Mr. Nixon stated that "injecting the global strategic rivalry into the region is incompatible with Middle East peace and with détente in U.S.-Soviet relations."[36] If the cease-fire could be sustained and Soviet military intervention curbed, Washington hoped that both Arabs and Israelis might become more flexible, the former be-cause they had no option but to negotiate and the latter because their military supremacy would be assured.

The Soviet-Egyptian connection was actually much weaker than the United States presumed at the time. Already by spring 1971, Sadat and the Kremlin had become wary of one another's intentions and fidelity. The immediate cause was the proposal on April 17 to unite Egypt, Libya and Syria in a Federation of Arab Republics to which the Sudan later asked to accede; Aly Sabry and the pro-Soviet faction opposed the union, whereupon Sadat forestalled a coup by imprisoning Sabry and his supporters, especially those in the KGB-influenced secret police.[37] The

Soviet-Egyptian "friendship and cooperation" pact was then pressed suddenly on Sadat by Soviet President Podgorny in a dramatic two-day visit. Its signing on May 27, 1971, coming within weeks of Secretary Rogers' visit, deepened Washington's suspicions without increasing pressure on Israel. The Sabry episode, the friendship pact and the unsuccessful communist coup in the Sudan during June convinced Sadat that Moscow and its military advisors were far from neutral in Arab domestic affairs.[38]

The risks of Soviet subversion might have been more tolerable to Cairo if the relationship with Moscow had been yielding political advantages. Instead there was stalemate. The Egyptian government greatly feared the "no war/no peace" situation produced by the cease-fire and diplomatic stagnation. Unless a victory of some sort appeared near, Egypt's "mobilized inactivity." with the country's manpower and economy devoted perpetually to a war without battles, made no sense. Soviet pressure on the United States represented Egypt's major hope for upsetting the Israeli occupation, but this hope lacked force without military action to sustain it. Toward the end of 1971, Sadat tried to agitate both Moscow and Washington. He declared 1971 to be the "Year of Decision," denounced the cease-fire on November 20 and demanded more advanced weaponry from the U.S.S.R.

Soviet use of Egyptian facilities to assist India in the war against Muslim Pakistan in late 1971 and Washington's linkage of the Middle East dispute to détente in early 1972 made Moscow's position untenable. Sadat was left dangling ignominiously as the "Year of Decision" ended without Egyptian military action or Israeli withdrawal. Already in early 1972, the Egyptian president was blaming the Soviets publicly for the miscarriage of his plans, for their failure to supply him advanced aircraft equal to Israel's Phantoms, and for their use of Egypt as a base to pursue purely Soviet interests.[39] The political and financial burden of the Soviet "presence" had become unbearable.

The Nixon-Brezhnev summit conference in May 1972 brought the two superpowers no closer to agreement on the Middle East, though a series of strategic arms accords were reached (SALT I) and a Declaration of Principles was signed. Initial press reports suggested that the Soviets refused to restrain their attempt to create a major strategic base in Egypt or to agree to any regional arms control measures. [40] But the entire summit, which had taken place despite Washington's Vietnam bombing policy, suggested to Cairo that Moscow's refusal to satisfy Egypt's arms requests had been "codified." The Declaration of Principles in particular pledged the signatories to avoid confrontation, to exercise restraint and to consult frequently.

Time was running out for Sadat. The military and diplomatic stalemate, general resentment of the Soviet role, army unrest, and the cost of the Soviet establishment (Egypt paid in hard currency) threatened Sadat's authority and Egypt's solvency. Public criticism of the Soviet role by *Al-Ahram* publisher Muhammad Hassanain Heikal and War Minister Muhammad Ahmed Sadek brought complaints from Moscow but no answer to Sadat's persistent demands for further weaponry. [41] On July 7, 1972, Sadat expelled or "terminated" the services of all Soviet personnel, reclaimed the military bases previously under exclusive Soviet control and requested a new formulation of the Egyptian-Soviet relationship.

The circumstances of the expulsion order suggested a desperate gesture rather than a well-conceived strategy. The timing was wretched. It had long been axiomatic in Arab reckoning that the United States could do nothing against Israel during an American presidential campaign, and Nixon was then waging his expensive effort to defeat George McGovern. Furthermore, the immediate impact of the gesture was the reverse of that desired: both the United States and Israel now expected Sadat to become more flexible because he was weaker.

Premier Meir's offer to resume negotiations on an interim accord to reopen the Suez Canal in return for "direct talks" was contemptuously refused by Sadat. He appealed to the United States: despite American agreement that an Israeli withdrawal was a prerequisite to peace, why had Washington refused to "deliver" Israel, thereby facilitating the Jarring mission and Secretary Rogers' peace initiatives? This was indeed a dramatic turn of events. Instead of Soviet assistance and American acquiescence in the war against Israel, Egypt now sought American intervention on behalf of the Arab cause.

The Soviet expulsion achieved one of Washington's major objectives. It was interpreted accurately as the product of a military stalemate and détente policy. But both the United States and Israel misjudged the significance of the apparent end of Cairo's military option and mistook the complex constraints from which Sadat was struggling to free himself. Initially, Soviet participation in the war of attrition gave Egypt a deterrent against total military defeat. The Egyptians then sought to convert this deterrence into an offensive force, believing that Soviet aircraft and missile systems could harass the Israeli Air Force sufficiently to give Egypt's numerical superiority a decisive opportunity. Once Cairo was committed to this strategy, Moscow's reluctance to play the offensive role assigned it for larger Soviet political reasons (détente) effectively canceled the war option. The expulsion maneuver was therefore less significant to Egyptian military proficiency than it was to overall Egyptian strategy.[42] Cairo would try to isolate the decision to make war from the U.S.-Soviet détente by reducing local Soviet leverage and increasing Arab war potential. If Soviet strategic aircraft were unavailable, a new military strategy would have to be devised.

The United States and Israel have been severely criticized—since the Yom Kippur War—for not having availed themselves of the opportunity presented by the Soviet expulsion. A "generous" offer, it is alleged, could have deflected Sadat from the war option, eliminated the need for any Soviet arms and perhaps begun the long road toward peace. This retrospective critique reads back the reality and impressions of the post-1973 war period to the events and perceptions of 1972.

As stated earlier, the Egyptian maneuver was timed badly; it was also interpreted correctly as a sign of weakness. But Sadat's weakness did not make the Egyptian diplomatic position more flexible: Cairo still insisted that Resolution 242 required total Israeli withdrawal and that the prerequisite to indirect negotiations, preferably through the UN or the great powers, was Israeli accession to this interpretation. The course chosen by the Egyptians—Arab self-help—meant closer ties with the even more politically rigid Libyans and Syrians. Trapped as he was between the extremists of the new Federation of Arab Republics and the quarrel with Moscow, there were good grounds for questioning Sadat's reliability and longevity.

For the United States to have done what the critics demanded necessitated a complete turn: pressure on Israel for concessions in order to reward Egypt for doing what it had been forced to do by American-Israeli policies. The only peace plan "on the table"—the Rogers formula for an interim agreement—was unacceptable to both sides, though more offensive to Israel for two reasons: first, it required linkage of the interim agreement to a larger settlement involving more Israeli withdrawal without a correspondingly clear Arab political commitment; second, it gave Egypt the right to station soldiers (even if a limited number) in the vacated areas, thereby prejudicing the Israeli demand for a demilitarized Sinai. Beyond these details, direct mediation rendered the whole Rogers policy inherently objectionable to Premier Meir. Once the military pressure posed by the Soviet presence subsided, the Israeli government reverted to its preferred position.

Thus there was no political or military reason for the United States to press her luck in yet another Middle East quarrel without evidence of significant diplomatic change on either side. The U.S. election campaign also reduced Washington's interest. President Nixon depicted the Middle East stalemate and the Soviet reverse as a triumph for his firm and active policy. Secretary Rogers pressed on to the melancholy conclusion of his interim agreement scheme: a UN speech in October. Since the Egyptian political position appeared to harden as Cairo's military position seemed to weaken, Washington reverted to "watchful waiting." As it turned out, watchful waiting became malign neglect. The United States had devised a successful policy to deal with one Egyptian strategy and with the Soviet attempt to manipulate this strategy for its own purposes. But the assumption that no other Egyptian option existed, based on reasoning imported from Jerusalem, bore constant re-examination. After fall 1972, this assumption met fewer objections even as its validity declined.

The Arab Strategy: Evolution of the Oil Weapon

Sadat's expulsion of the Soviet advisers during the summer of 1972 broke decisively with Nasser's foreign policy of alliance with the East in order to neutralize the West. Détente clearly precluded tactics based on the era of confrontation, and though Moscow might still be needed for war, only Washington possessed sufficient authority over Israel to compel her withdrawal. The United States respected strength but was bound to oppose Soviet intervention; hence, the main strength in the future had to be Arab. In recruiting Arab strength, Sadat faced severe problems of flexibility and timing. He could not engage Washington's serious attention with Premier Qaddafi's opinions, Syrian opposition to Resolution 242 or the Palestine Liberation Organization's terror tactics. Egypt's economic and political resources did not allow for indefinite mobilization.

Sadat was therefore forced to break with Nasser's other major policies as well. He loosened Nasser's bureaucratic socialism in the hope of improving the country's deteriorating financial position. More importantly, he journeyed to Saudi Arabia and the Gulf states to reconcile with King Faisal and the oil sheiks and to gain their support the a new political offensive aimed at Washington.[43]

King Faisal's views on the Arab-Israeli dispute were unique. He believed that communism and Zionism were partners in a joint atheistic plan to conquer the world, against which were ranged the Islamic and Christian states. Saudi society had to be protected against such influences, and this could best be done through alliance with the more powerful Western nations, particularly the United States. Faisal had always been reluctant to employ political pressure through the oil weapon against his necessary patron in Washington. In addition, there was a practical reason: the tactic had never worked.

An oil embargo had been launched against Britain and France

in 1956, and against the United States and Britain in 1967. Coupled with the closure of the Suez Canal and the Arabian pipelines, roughly three-quarters of the oil destined for Western Europe had been cut off. But these actions were thwarted by the variety of sources and surplus of supply that has always troubled the oil business. Moreover, the great multinational oil companies and the consumer governments had cooperated sufficiently to spread around the temporary reduction in supply, and store up a reserve sufficient to prevent immediate economic disaster. Given the falling real price of oil during the late 1950s and early 1960s because of new discoveries and massive reserves, the Saudi government and its Persian Gulf friends could not finance an embargo and the Arab war effort simultaneously. Finally, there were more elemental fears: unilateral attempts to dictate oil supplies had provoked joint U.S.-European political pressure in the past, including "gunboat diplomacy."

By 1972 many of these obstacles to a successful embargo no longer existed. European political influence had virtually disappeared. The British and French military bases were gone, and their empires were history. The great economic growth of Western Europe, Japan and the United States during the 1960s exceeded all estimates of energy consumption,[44] eliminating the strategic Western Hemisphere emergency alternative to Middle East oil supplies.

The relationship between the major oil companies and the producer countries had also changed. This was due partly to the oil surplus of the early 1960s and the efforts of the smaller, independent oil companies to develop their own sources of crude oil. In the ensuing competition, the major companies cut the "posted price," an artificial figure used to calculate taxes, which had been designed to protect the producer governments against the downward pressure of surplus.

These cuts, which threatened the financial stability of the oil-exporting countries, led directly to the formation of the Organization of Petroleum-Exporting Countries (OPEC) in 1960. It proved singularly useless for most of the next decade, unable to influence the posted price and adept only at issuing manifestoes ignored by the oil corporations. The Libyan revolution of 1969[45] and the rapid tightening of the supply/demand situation soon made OPEC more important. The new Libyan government arbitrarily raised prices at the expense of Occidental Oil, one of the larger independents. Since Libya was the sole source of Occidental's crude, the major corporations were not eager to bail out this unwanted independent; furthermore, the French and Italian national oil companies saw an opportunity to improve their own crude-poor positions at the expense of the "Anglo-Saxon" monopoly.[46]

Lacking the market conditions and political support of the past, the "majors" struggled hard to protect their Middle East agreements from any leapfrog phenomenon after the successful Libyan price increase. They demanded to negotiate with OPEC. The producer countries refused, and in this atmosphere negotiations with the Persian Gulf states began in Teheran. Two issues were paramount: the companies wished to stabilize the company-country relationships against Libyan-style tactics, and the countries wished to protect themselves against the surplus everyone expected sooner or later. The agreement that emerged on February 14, 1971, provided for doubling the Persian Gulf states' "take" over the 1971-1975 period; posted prices were boosted immediately by 35 percent. By pinning the profit-sharing mechanism on the posted rather than the market price "the Teheran Agreement protected the governments against *falling* market prices, but not against *rising* market prices, the expectation shared by both companies and governments being that posted prices would remain above market prices."[47]

The Teheran Agreement had been advertised by the oil companies as expensive but "stabilizing." After the international monetary crisis, which brought about the U.S. dollar's devaluation in December 1971, however, the agreement became more expensive and less stable. Early in 1972 it was revised to increase the posted price another 8.5 percent (Persian Gulf oil still sold for less than $2.50 a barrel). Negotiations were also begun between firms and the governments of Saudi Arabia, Qatar, Kuwait, Iraq and Abu Dhabi on shared ownership or "participation." More significantly, Iraq seized the Iraq Petroleum Company on June 1. Though the IPC was owned by a consortium of U.S., British, Dutch and French firms, the majors could no longer organize a boycott of the nationalized oil after the French and Italian government-owned companies signed long-term agreements with the Iraqi government. Thus, the international oil corporations found themselves increasingly unable to resist demands for higher taxes and greater control over production rates.

The Teheran Agreement, weakened already by the dollar's troubles, was undermined further by the dramatic American need for imported oil. This surprised Washington badly. In February 1970 President Nixon's Special Cabinet Task Force on Imports expected the United States to import a maximum of 5 million barrels daily by 1980, most of which could come from Venezuela; they recommended that imports from the Middle East be limited to 10 percent of total petroleum supply. [48] But by 1973, total U.S. oil imports already exceeded this level, comprising more than 25 percent of total oil consumption, with Middle East (or Eastern Hemisphere) sources supplying 20 percent. The cause was to be found primarily in the substitution of petroleum for natural gas, whose low regulated price stimulated demand far in excess of supply. [49] As a consequence, American energy consumption would derive increasingly from oil, *even if consumption trends were reduced*. Thus, American oil imports averaged 4.7 million barrels a day in 1972, including 800,000 from the Middle East; one year later, imports had risen 32 percent to 6 million barrels a day, with 1.2 million barrels from the Middle East.

The American entry into the Middle East oil market, the overheated, inflationary economies of the major Atlantic countries and Japan, and the dollar devaluation produced a radical change. Already in 1972, the oil-producing countries were selling their participation crude at good prices. The majors began to refuse long-term commitments to third-party purchasers (that is, the independents), enlarging the "spot market"; this in turn bid up the market price. As the market price approached and then surpassed the posted price, the profit split worked in favor of the companies, defeating the whole purpose of the Teheran Agreement.[50]

This seller's market, particularly the prospect that future American economic growth would depend on Middle East oil, significantly strengthened the oil weapon in two ways. First, the Saudi Arabian government could pressure Washington without threatening a production cutback or embargo. Second, the Arab oil producers, particularly those with small populations such as Saudi Arabia and Kuwait, had more than enough cash to forgo increased revenues, finance Arab war preparations and even to consider an embargo if need be. The oil weapon was thus a by-product of a consumption and pricing trend that had developed independently of the Arab-Israeli war.

The Egyptian-Soviet Reconciliation

The oil weapon, which could not be grasped successfully by Egypt until Nasser's Pan-Arab legacy had been discarded, was not the only instrument sought by Sadat. American intervention, not acquiescence, was now the goal. This could not be obtained by making war to destroy the state of Israel. Instead, the war's purposes would have to be aimed directly at the principal weakness in the U.S.-Israeli relationship: their differing positions on the extent of withdrawal and border changes. Washington might be expected to help Israel if her existence were at stake; to spare Israel the pains of a war over occupied territory, especially if an oil embargo threatened vital American economic and political interests elsewhere, was less likely.

Ironically, this new position coincided precisely with the military advice offered by Moscow for years: the Arab states could not defeat Israel militarily, but they might inflict a costly blow sufficient to dislodge the political stalemate in their favor. How to turn this possibility into pressure on Washington had been the great issue that eventually upset the Egyptian-Soviet alliance created during the war of attrition. The answer was deceptively simple: wage an Arab-financed war to recover occupied territory, to shake American and Israeli confidence and to restore Arab morale, and do all of this without a massive Soviet military presence.

Since the Egyptian military machine was still Soviet-made, Sadat had the delicate task of approaching Moscow even as he preached Arab self-reliance. Moscow proved receptive to a new deal, especially one that endorsed Soviet military assumptions, renewed influence in Cairo through an arms supply and avoided demands that might disturb Soviet-American détente. In February the deal was initiated when a Soviet military mission visited Cairo. By April 1973 Sadat was expressing public satisfaction over the Soviet weapons supplied to Egypt and Syria.[51] He should have been satisfied: Egypt and Syria were obtaining weaponry not yet distributed to Warsaw Pact countries, including a more substantial anti-aircraft SAM system and a strategic deterrent to replace Soviet aircraft—Scud-B missiles.[52] But Moscow still warned the Arabs against rash behavior during the summer of 1973, "rash" being defined as expecting to defeat Israel in battle or involve the Soviet Union in a confrontation.[53] To ensure this, the Soviets kept their clients' munitions and equipment stocks at a level adequate only for a limited war.[54]

If postwar military recollections are of any value, the Soviets should not have worried. Egypt and Syria were simply planning a military operation of a scale and type long advocated by Moscow and long rehearsed by the Arab armies. On November 18, 1973, Egyptian War Minister Lt. General Ahmad Ismail Aly discussed publicly his prewar estimates of Israeli strengths and weaknesses, especially Israel's sensitivity to losses, her long supply lines, economic inability to wage a long war and "overweening arrogance." The Arab strategy simply intended to take advantage of the "overweening arrogance" and excessive Israeli confidence by launching a surprise attack to inflict maximum losses.[55]

While the military and economic weapons were being prepared, the Egyptians also launched political initiatives designed to isolate Israel and justify the war. Sadat's national security adviser, Hafez Ismail, visited London, Bonn, Moscow, Washington and the

United Nations in early 1973, stating that Egypt would not enter direct talks but wished to resume some sort of negotiations. It is difficult to determine the seriousness of this effort; Israel had agreed to "proximity talks" before, and a strong effort could probably have brought Mrs. Meir around again, if the offer seemed sincere. In any event, Ismail's mission came to nothing and did not prevent Washington's sale of more Phantoms to Israel in March. The Egyptians were spared the justification of their case by the entire turn of Israeli politics during 1973, and isolating Israel from Western Europe and Africa proved to be easy.

The Illusions of 1973

The expulsion of the Soviet advisers from Egypt in the summer of 1972 put Israel greatly at ease. Premier Meir's policy, which appeared at one point to be drawing the country into a military confrontation with Moscow and a political crisis with Washington, had paid off handsomely. Though still without Arab political recognition, Israel was at the height of her military authority, maintaining far-flung military outposts with a small army, a technologically superior air force and an expanding local arms industry. Israel's burgeoning strength was buttressed further by the practical achievement of a long sought goal: the greatest international power, the United States, looked on Israel's security as an essential factor in relations with the Soviet Union. While Washington did not underwrite a permanent Israeli occupation of the Sinai, the Golan Heights or the Jordan Valley, the United States was resolutely opposed to any violent challenge to that occupation, especially an attack encouraged by Moscow.

In this heady atmosphere the government of Golda Meir grew careless. Suggestions by friendly Americans and Europeans that Israel should sponsor a peace initiative or at least reach a consensus on her essential geographic demands—which would have been useful, if only for propaganda purposes—were met by the well-worn formula of "negotiations without preconditions." The dangers of the SAM anti-aircraft missiles to Israeli air superiority, the difficulties of defense with small, immobile garrisons against huge standing forces, the long supply lines and reliance on civilian transport, the axioms about short wars and great-power stakes in preventing Arab defeat—all of these could be studied as factors of the past. The Arabs would not make war unless they could be confident of victory; they could not be confident of victory without air superiority and full Soviet support; air superiority was not within the technical competence of Arab air forces, and the Soviets would not support a war in view of their détente with Washington. As Defense Minister Dayan put it on January 30, 1972, six months before the Soviet expulsion, the Arabs would "have to plan to push us back with ground forces and, if they are to dream of succeeding, an immense air force." [56]

In the winter of 1972-1973 Israel devoted her ingenuity not to devising peace plans but instead to combating international terrorism. Beginning with the September 1972 Munich Massacre, the Palestinian guerrillas, balked on the battlefield, attempted to disrupt international air travel and to attack Israeli installations abroad. Many Arab governments assisted this campaign with money, arms and passports; all of them except Jordan applauded the various massacres of civilians perpetuated by the Black September squad of the Palestine Liberation Organization. [57] The Israelis—and the United States—were surprised to find the West European states and the Japanese government unwilling to offend Arab sensibilities by concerted international measures against the terrorist bases, their sanctuaries and their financial sources. More than eighty terrorists imprisoned during 1972-1973 were released after further hijackings and threats.

The European governments were also modifying their political positions on the Middle East, with the pro-Arab stand advocated by Paris gaining strength. Part of this could be laid to Common Market politics; in their desire to enter the EEC and overcome French opposition, the British found their "neutral" Middle East policy expendable. More of it may have derived from the terrorist campaign, an impending sense of the energy crisis and a general feeling that Israel, as the superior power, should do "more" to stimulate negotiations.

Whatever the reason, Israel simply dismissed the West Europeans as politically and morally impotent after their feeble reaction to the terrorists. [58] So long as European Community trade negotiations remained free of political bias, the Israelis would rely on their West German friends to protect their interests. But this too was changing. When Chancellor Willy Brandt, with his personal record of opposition to the Nazis, paid a visit to Israel in June 1973, he explained gently to his hosts that West German entry into the UN, *Ostpolitik* and the passage of the war generation dictated a more normal relationship with Israel. "Normal relations of a special character," a singularly ambiguous phrase, was the chancellor's description of future German-Israeli dealings. The Israeli leadership, weighed down perhaps by tragic memories, refused to countenance any change in the Federal Republic's attitude. [59]

Israel's deteriorating diplomatic relations with the major West European countries were not the only political costs of the stalemate. The highly successful Israeli effort to cultivate diplomatic friends in Africa, an effort also distinguished by effective technical assistance and a favorable trade balance, proved no barrier to Arab pressure. The growing financial diplomacy used by the North African Arab states, an attractive propaganda campaign, the failure of the OAU mediation committee on behalf of the Jarring mission in 1971, and a certain African propensity to retain the Israeli technical missions regardless of diplomatic relations rapidly reversed Israeli positions throughout Africa. [60] The actual rupture of diplomatic relations began with Uganda in 1972 and several of the French-speaking countries in 1972-1973—all cases that could be explained away as the product of bizarre personalities (such as Idi Amin) or as a reflection of French foreign policy. Unlike the European situation, which had already been discounted by Jerusalem, the extraordinary behavior of the African states later in the year was very much a surprise.

Israel's growing diplomatic isolation was accompanied by

other signs of impending conflict, some of which should have been noticed by the United States. May 1973 proved to be particularly rich in both warnings of the impending catastrophe and the stout resolution of the victims to pursue their illusions. On May 3, President Nixon issued his foreign policy report to the Congress, subtitled *Shaping a Durable Peace*. The most self-congratulatory of all the Nixon reports, it stressed the significant progress made on the "global structure of peace"—the Vietnam settlement, the SALT agreements, the opening to China, the summit talks, the "adjustment" of partnership with Europe and Japan through economic negotiations. The Middle East was depicted as quiet but dangerous; great-power commitments to avoid confrontation were emphasized. The president promised to make a maximum effort on the Middle East in the forthcoming year. Summarizing the international situation in his introduction, Nixon wrote: "A changed world has moved closer to a lasting peace. Many events were colorful, but their true drama is that they can herald a new epoch, not fade as fleeting episodes."[61]

That same day in Riyadh, Saudi Arabia, a colorful event was indeed heralding a new epoch. Amid the incense of the royal court, King Faisal told the president of ARAMCO, Frank Jungers, that the United States had to change the "direction of events" in the Middle East. The king's aide elaborated later that Egypt would renew hostilities in the hope of pressuring Israel into "meaningful negotiations," even though the military situation was hopeless.[62] Later, on May 23 in Geneva, Faisal warned the ARAMCO management again; he had just visited Cairo, and he could not allow Saudi Arabia to become isolated because of American inaction.[63] The oil executives passed on the message publicly and privately.

For Israel, May began triumphantly with a massive military parade in Jerusalem to celebrate the country's twenty-fifth anniversary. It was an expensive and controversial gesture, which included a flyby of most of Israel's air force and a tank parade. Thereafter, the Israeli government was alarmed by reports of large troop concentrations near the Suez Canal. On May 10 Soviet Defense Minister Andrei Grechko began a four-day tour of Syria and then visited Cairo to sign a new defense pact (probably to supply the Scud missiles). An aerial display put on by the Egyptians was followed on May 16 by a MiG-23 overflight of the Sinai that Israeli Phantoms were unable to intercept. A partial and expensive mobilization was ordered (costing $10 million), despite the prediction of Intelligence Chief Eliahu Zeira that these were only seasonal maneuvers; nothing happened. This incident confirmed Israel's belief that Egyptian strategy still depended on a challenge to Israeli air supremacy, a challenge only possible if Soviet-piloted aircraft joined the battle, a development precluded by détente. On May 21, two days after Sadat visited Damascus, Defense Minister Dayan closed the incident with a vaguely prophetic warning to the General Staff Branch: "Gentlemen, please be prepared for war when those who threaten us are Egypt and Syria." [64]

Washington remained strangely sanguine. On May 1 the United States removed all quantitative controls of crude oil imports, putting further pressure on a tight market and supplying additional arguments for a revision of the Teheran Agreement and the potency of the oil weapon. The Nixon administration was attending to other matters. The United States and her West European allies had just gone through a very difficult period, marked by bitter controversy over trade and monetary arrangements. The Smithsonian Agreement of 1971 had collapsed after the lifting of Phase-2 controls from the U.S. economy in early 1973, and inflation was rampant once more. On the political front, the European and Japanese governments had been surprised and very unhappy about the timing, process and some of the details emerging from the Moscow and Peking summits. [65] Hoping to improve Atlantic relationships, Kissinger had delivered his "Year of Europe" speech on April 23, which called *inter alia* for a joint Atlantic approach to the energy problem. But an EEC meeting on May 23 in Brussels took no action on this proposal, leaving each state to pursue its own energy policies, a situation that prevailed up to the war and during it.

While his assistant for national security affairs tried to revive a constructive dialogue with America's allies, President Nixon busied himself with Watergate strategy and preparations for Brezhnev's forthcoming June visit, when the United States and the U.S.S.R. would agree to "immediately enter into urgent consultations with others" should a situation develop that might invoke the risk of nuclear conflict. [66] On the whole, Nixon and Kissinger were pleased with their handiwork, which included the Paris peace accords in January, settling the Vietnam war. On May 19, Armed Forces Day, Nixon declared to a naval audience: "In the explosive Middle East, we averted a major crisis in 1970. . . . There are still enormously difficult problems there and in other parts of the world, but we have come a long way over the past five years toward building a structure of peace in the world— much further simply than ending a long war, but building a structure that will avoid other wars. . . ." [67] On May 23 Kissinger amplified this satisfaction with "structural" progress, telling C.L. Sulzberger of the *New York Times*: "Our foreign policy has been painfully built up so that now all the pieces are in place. We are at last in a position to reap the fruits." [68]

The only jarring note in this litany was delivered by Assistant Secretary of State Joseph Sisco in a May 7 speech to pro-Israeli groups celebrating that state's twenty-fifth anniversary. Sisco declared that the "no war/no peace" situation was inherently unsatisfactory. He criticized the Arab and and Israeli "desire to have it both ways, to have their cake and eat it too, to keep their options open." This, he said, needed to be replaced by a consensus in Israel and the Arab states over priorities in the exchange of territory for peace, as formulated by Resolution 242. The myths of implacable Israeli expansionism and implacable Arab desires to destroy Israel, among others, should be jettisoned so that the "history of lost opportunities" for Middle East peace could be concluded. Sisco closed by stressing American determination to move the Middle East toward settlement, stating: "In our judgment, the chasm on an overall settlement is too broad to bridge in one jump. But practical step-by-step progress is feasible, beginning with negotiations on an agreement for some Israeli withdrawal in Sinai, the reopening of the Suez Canal, and an extended cease-fire." [69]

Sisco's speech did not impress the Israelis, who were in no mood for State Department lectures on lost opportunities. While bewildered and angry over diplomatic reverses and the terrorist campaign, Israel remained supremely confident of long-term stability. After May 1973 international developments assumed less importance than domestic political disputes. Premier Meir had announced months earlier her intention to retire before the next general election, scheduled for October 29. Political intrigues soon immobilized her administration, and the leadership quarrel was aggravated by mounting strife over Israeli policy toward the occupied territories.

This policy had been shaped by two concerns: the need to keep peace and the role of the territories in the government's negotiating strategy. At Dayan's insistence, the Arabs had been permitted to work in Israel and to maintain contacts with Arab states, including travel across the Jordan River. Politicking remained severely restricted. This strategy of "open bridges" helped to pacify the population, especially as Arab military prospects declined. It did not settle the issue of the future disposition of the areas, which were supposedly governed by the "negotiations without preconditions" slogan. In 1968 Deputy Premier Yigal Allon had proposed a plan of eventual settlement, based mainly on a bizarre mixture of security lines, commercial corridors and "strategic" Jewish settlements throughout the West Bank, but the plan was laid aside. Instead Israel justified her forty-four settlements and 5,000 pioneers in the Golan, West Bank and Sinai areas as either temporary security measures, bargaining cards or "signs" to the Arabs that delayed negotiations meant less to negotiate over.

The growing role of Arab labor in Israel's economy, the infusion of wealth into the traditional communities of the West Bank and the high Arab birth rate presented important problems for Israel. Arguing the case for long-term stability, Dayan sought increasing economic integration and demanded that Jews be allowed to buy land in the occupied areas. In his view, integration hardly affected negotiations with the Arab states; the Arabs either rejected negotiations out of pride or believed that the size of the Arab population would prevent Israel from absorbing the territory.

This was a devastating critique of the government's unproductive political strategy and an argument for eventual annexation. It was opposed strenuously by Allon, Finance Minister Pinhas Sapir and Foreign Minister Abba Eban on economic, demographic and diplomatic grounds. To prevent a disastrous party split, Mrs. Meir agreed to stand again for the premiership. The land purchase issue was compromised through the so-called Galilee Protocol (published August 22, 1973), which essentially endorsed Dayan's proposals and then proceeded to qualify them heavily: land sales were to be approved only by special government action, and the other economic projects would be financed by none other than Pinhas Sapir. The finance minister knew well that inflation-ridden Israel would have little money for these enterprises after the elections; he agreed readily to the compromise. The Galilee Protocol was a recipe for bad press and government paralysis; it embarrassed the United States and gave the Arab states a valuable propaganda argument that the "no war/no peace" situation was a formula for Israeli annexation.

The Nixon administration was also beset by political troubles in the summer of 1973. The increasingly compelling Watergate affair already gave signs of eroding the president's prestige as the press and Congress explored the connections between the burglars and the White House. It was difficult to discern the affair's impact on foreign policy. The carefully staged play pieces of détente, especially Brezhnev's visit to the United States in June, and Nixon's aura of success and competence in foreign affairs were weighed against his administration's shaky economic performance and his personal reputation for underhanded tactics. This political schizophrenia probably protected Washington's foreign policy; as the presidential crisis deepened, the consensus grew that national security interests abroad should not be undermined by domestic opposition.

Kissinger, the presidential adviser largely credited with Nixon's international successes, was the immediate beneficiary. His nomination as secretary of state during August was universally interpreted as a maneuver by Nixon to shore up presidential prestige, since it had long been assumed that Kissinger carried more influence than Secretary of State Rogers. In retrospect, this explanation seems peculiar; the new secretary of state's reputation was bound to undermine Nixon's final argument, put in raw form at his last visit to Moscow in 1974, that he (Nixon) was indispensable to world peace. Kissinger himself felt absolutely certain that whatever the immediate appearance, the diminution of presidential authority had to affect the conduct of foreign policy. During May—the month of illusions—he told Sulzberger that "the effect of Watergate—if it hasn't ended soon—is bound to be felt in autumn." But he also believed that Watergate would not stimulate miscalculation in the Middle East. [70]

The new nominee lost no time in tackling, or appearing to tackle, the Middle East problem. Characteristically, Kissinger began with a "media event"; the first Jewish secretary of state invited all the Arab UN ambassadors to dine and consult, implying publicly and privately that American initiatives were imminent. Later, he recalled: "I remember saying then that I recognized that the situation in the Middle East was intolerable for the Arab nations; I pledged that the United States would involve itself actively in the search for a just and lasting peace. . . . I gave my personal promise to make a special effort to begin concrete steps toward peace." [71] These assurances did not impress the Arab delegates, and if Washington felt any urgency about the situation, neither the president nor his secretary of state conveyed that impression successfully to the local parties or the Soviets in September 1973.

Why the Surprise

Both Israel and the United States, then, spent the immediate months before the war concentrating on their respective domestic politics. Jerusalem rested on its military superiority, preferring to postpone the pressing disturbances of the leadership dispute, the territorial issue and the loss of international political support.

Washington was transfixed by the twin questions of presidential culpability and authority; foreign affairs were thought to be well in hand.

The events of 1972-1973 as recounted here, however, revealed a disturbing series of illusions held by the United States and Israel concerning Egyptian strategy, détente, the oil weapon and the European position. As signs of impending disturbance mounted, so the illusions deepened and widened, to be cherished until the day of war itself. The surprise of the war derived from a systematic misinterpretation of events and not a few mistaken impressions. These events and the misinterpretations were the following:

(1) *The change in Egyptian strategy signified by the Soviet expulsion in 1972.* Unable to bring the Soviets to war with Israel on Egypt's behalf and unwilling to risk negotiation without a military option, Sadat finally had to choose between an eventual coup and a war with limited objectives. Washington and Jerusalem did not believe that such a limited war was politically or militarily feasible.

(2) *The role of détente signified by Moscow's refusal to supply advanced weaponry to Egypt.* Incapable of broadening its appeal to Egypt beyond the arms supply, unwilling to jeopardize its promising relationship with the United States, and unsuccessful in promoting Israeli withdrawal through the war of attrition, Moscow finally had to choose between a larger military intervention in Egypt or a different relationship with Cairo. The United States and Israel did not believe that the Soviet Union could successfully assist an Egyptian battle plan without a larger military intervention, especially in the air; it was thought that such an intervention—or any encouragement of an Arab war—was precluded by the détente and the general pattern of Soviet behavior after the 1972 Moscow summit.

(3) *The potential of the oil weapon signified by Saudi warnings.* The dependency of Western Europe and Japan on Middle East oil, the entry of the United States on the "Eastern Hemisphere" market, the tight supply situation of 1973, the extraordinary consumption requirements projected by economic trends, and the consequent strength of the oil producers gave the Arab oil producers sufficient money and strategic opportunity to finance a war and an embargo simultaneously. The United States, Israel, the West European governments and Japan believed that diversity of supply, the

failure of past embargoes and the revenue needs of the oil producers reduced the chances of an embargo or the linkage of market conditions to the Arab-Israeli dispute.

(4) *The gap between the American and West European positions on the Middle East.* The general lack of coherent cooperation among the Atlantic allies in resolving fundamental economic issues during 1969-1973, differing reactions to terrorism, Israel's loss of European support, and European appreciation that the United States could no longer provide an alternative energy source burdened the Atlantic Alliance with strongly divergent interests. The United States underestimated the extent of the European "defection," and Israel dismissed the European influence as irrelevant.

Taken together, these four factors fatally reduced American and Israeli deterrence to prevent war. They also meant that Egypt was planning a limited action aimed at upsetting the political stalemate—using a Soviet military plan, Moscow's support and the oil embargo—in order to surprise and demoralize Israel and to force the United States into the dispute to the benefit of the Arab cause. Taken separately, however, each of these developments did not appear to undermine the Middle East stalemate. Furthermore, they lent themselves easily to erroneous preconceptions. Egyptian strategy could be dismissed as the futile gestures of desperation; the Soviets were "quarantined" safely by détente, unable to encourage a successful war; the oil weapon was sheer bluff, explained by the wearisome complexities of Arab rivalries; the Atlantic partnership was soundly established despite the noise of temporary discord. Israel's political immobility and military overconfidence, America's misconceptions concerning the effect of détente in limiting Soviet flexibility, indifference toward the oil situation, and careless confidence in the basic unity of Atlantic interests blinded the victims to the blows about to befall them.

2. CONFLICT AND DIPLOMACY

The War [72]

It is bad enough for governments to be surprised out of ignorance; it is far worse for governments to be surprised out of self-delusion. The final political event signifying the impending conflict—the sudden reconciliation of Hussein, Sadat and Assad in Cairo on September 12, 1973—did not alarm Jerusalem or Washington. When war broke out on the Day of Atonement, 10 Ramadan, October 6, 1973, the Israeli government (and the United States) had known of immense and menacing Egyptian and Syrian military concentrations for more than a week. [73] Israeli Intelligence Chief Zeira, Chief of Staff David Elazar and Defense Minister Dayan were comforted by their experience of the false alarm in May and by their knowledge that the enemy's air forces were inferior. Premier Meir had been in Europe, trying unsuccessfully to persuade the Austrian government not to close the transit camp for Soviet Jews after a terrorist incident. When the premier returned on Wednesday, October 3, she was informed of the situation and told that the military recommended nothing be done. The issue was not discussed at the cabinet meeting that day.

On Thursday evening, a more ominous event was observed.

Soviet embassy personnel were airlifted from Damascus under emergency conditions. Since both Israeli and American intelligence analysts were thoroughly convinced that war was unlikely in view of Arab military weakness, the airlift was inexplicable; the Israelis and Secretary Kissinger ingeniously supposed that it indicated a new Arab-Soviet quarrel.[74]

The Israeli high command had worked out a formula for reinforcing its troops along the Suez Canal and the Golan Heights according to a "ratio of forces" with the Arab armies. The expense of partial mobilization in May and the unfailing confidence of General Zeira apparently led General Elazar and the minister of defense to ignore this ratio during the week preceding the war, except for strengthening the Golan Heights force on September 30 with an armored brigade. Nonetheless, the magnitude of the Arab build-up led to more intensive intelligence efforts on Friday morning, October 5, and an emergency cabinet meeting in Tel Aviv at noon.

The meeting was later to be a source of some controversy. Not all ministers were present, and even though he was in Tel Aviv, Treasury Minister Sapir "could not be found" in time. Those present agreed to give the power of emergency mobilization to the premier and minister of defense until the usual Sunday cabinet meeting. The secretary of the cabinet was instructed to ascertain where the ministers could be found over the Day of Atonement.

Very late that night, Israeli intelligence was informed by a trusted source that the Egyptians would attack the next day at 5:00 p.m. After further checking, Intelligence Chief Zeira conferred with Chief of Staff Elazar. On Saturday, October 6, at 6:00 a.m., the chief of staff urged Defense Minister Dayan to mobilize the Army of Israel and to attack the Arabs.

But Dayan opposed full mobilization. He seemed possessed of the curious fear that Israeli mobilization itself would lay his country open to the charge of provoking war. He was certain that a pre-emptive attack would jeopardize future American arms supplies to Israel.[75] There was undoubtedly strong feeling in the Israeli cabinet, based on the 1967 experience, that the Arabs should be seen clearly as the "aggressors" who began the war, but this reasoning only illustrated the Israeli government's extremely defective appreciation of foreign opinion. Not a single government besides the United States (and that only briefly) professed to be unduly disturbed by the fact that the Arabs attacked first; French Foreign Minister Jobert almost justified it as understandable in view of Israeli occupation.[76]

The defense minister finally agreed to a partial mobilization, in accordance with the ratio-of-forces doctrine. The air force had been on full alert since Friday, and the partial mobilization order should have dispatched armor and infantry to the southern and northern fronts. Instead, *no* mobilization order was issued.

The explanation for this bizarre delay may lie in the mobilization procedures and numbers involved, for General Elazar probably felt that he could persuade the premier to mobilize fully and attack. A partial mobilization might complicate Israel's rickety logistics system, unduly alarm the population and create political strife when ministers awoke to a military crisis.

It took three hours to convene a meeting between Mrs. Meir, Dayan and Elazar. At 10:00 a.m. the premier heard out the arguments on mobilization, dismissed Dayan's objections and ordered the chief of staff to proceed. But she refused a preemptive strike and informed the American ambassador of the government's moves. It was at this point, about 4:00 a.m. U.S. Eastern Daylight time, that the State Department learned of the Israeli moves. (Secretary Kissinger, then in New York for the UN General Assembly, was awakened only at 6:00 a.m., approximately two hours before the Arabs attacked.)[77] Mrs. Meir also called a cabinet meeting for noon.

In 1967 Israel had been fully mobilized for three weeks before the war began. The Israeli logistics system relied on civilian transport, and a plan to purchase and store trucks for the army had been eliminated for financial reasons. Given the assumption that Israel would have at least thirty-six hours notice before war broke out (the effective mobilization time), and her heavy investment in R&D and sophisticated aircraft, Israeli munitions stocks and transport arrangements in 1973 were designed essentially to fight the war of 1967. On October 6, 1973, Israel had only eight hours warning (though thought to be eleven hours), and the mobilization itself did not begin until four hours before the war; the lines of supply lay over greater distances and more difficult terrain than in 1967; and transport equipment did not include sufficient tank carriers and other critical vehicles. The result was chaos.

There were special problems on the Sinai front. Israeli strategy called for the rapid reinforcement of the Bar-Lev line, which was regarded as an early-warning system by some officers and a bona fide defense redoubt by others.[78] The commander of the southern front defenses was new to the job; he received orders or interpreted his orders to mean that he should not move up his reserve brigades until 4:00 p.m., lest the maneuver encourage the charge of "provocation" so feared by the Israeli government.[79] The result was that on October 6 fewer than fifty tanks and a thousand Israeli soldiers on the Bar-Lev line faced more than a thousand tanks and fifty thousand Egyptian soldiers.

At 2:00 p.m. the Egyptians and Syrians attacked. Their tactics differed. The Egyptian Army crossed the Suez Canal in an operation patiently practiced for several years. The infantry moved ahead of the tanks, which then consolidated. After gaining a few miles of ground, they stopped within range of the SAM missile installations to their rear. The Syrians used tanks to break through but soon lost coordination; armored forces came within a few kilometers of the edge of the Golan Heights, then turned back in search of infantry.

The Israelis knew within a few hours that the Bar-Lev line was lost. More menacing still were the reports of Syrian gains. Although the Jordanian front was still quiet, it posed a possible danger to Jerusalem. This meant that the preferred order of battle (to attack Egypt first while holding off the Syrians) had to be reversed: a holding action against the Egyptians (and Jordanians should they enter the war) and maximum force against the Syrians.

The Israelis rapidly discovered the price of their long supply lines, static defense and reliance on an exclusively air-armor team before full mobilization. The Israeli Air Force concentrated on ground support, and numerous jets were lost to the SAMs. The Sagger wire-guided anti-tank missiles used by the Egyptians required infantry action to dispel; several tank brigades were devastated before the requisite manpower could be assembled. Israel had to fight the first three days of the war without her customary concentration of force produced by rapid mobilization, with serious checks on her air superiority and armored mobility, with direct confrontation of the enemy's main forces instead of her favored war of maneuver, and with far greater expenditure of weapons and munitions than had ever been imagined. [80] The price of surprise was to fight the Arabs on their own terms.

The Israeli government soon showed the strain of the war. Convened at noon on Yom Kippur (October 6), the cabinet approved Premier Meir's decisions. Aside from Mrs. Meir, Dayan, Minister of Industry Chaim Bar-Lev and Minister without Portfolio Israel Galilee, the rest of the cabinet knew little of what was going on. The premier, as a senior Mapai Party leader, had opposed the national unity government forced on Levi Eshkol in 1967, saying that "Labour does not need partners in victory." This time she got her way; the opposition was left to oppose. With the whole population at war, the field was open to all sorts of rumors, the effects of which Mrs. Meir did not appreciate.

There were also prominent opposition figures in command positions. General Ariel Sharon, who had single-handedly brought together a shaky opposition coalition called the Likud before the war, had a major role on the southern front. When his nominal superior General Shmuel Gonen lost control of the situation out of either ignorance or shock, Sharon began to deal directly with Dayan. Bar-Lev, a former chief of staff, was dispatched by the cabinet to make sure that operations in the south bore a strong Mapai imprint. It was not too long before General Sharon's colorful condemnations of his military colleagues and political enemies were stirring anger against the premier and her one-party war policy. [81] Despite the surprise of the attack, the Israeli government still believed that the country's military prowess would reverse the situation within a few days. The high command also believed; on Monday, October 8, General Elazar publicly expressed his confidence that the national forces would soon destroy the enemy [82] and named the war the "War of the Day of Judgment." Within twenty-four hours, however, Elazar's own judgment was judged wanting. On October 9, his special assistant, Major General Aharon Yariv (former chief of intelligence), informed Israel and the world that the Bar-Lev line had been abandoned, that the war would not be short and that it was a war of attrition. [83]

Their original strategic concept destroyed, the Israeli military authorities improvised. Dayan, whose performance under duress has been severely criticized, apparently favored cutting losses on the southern front; other opinions prevailed. [84] Though taxed to the utmost, Israeli forces had already gained ground in Syria beyond the 1967 cease-fire and were pressing the Syrians toward Damascus. The strategy, such as it was, then prescribed a transfer of forces to the south to tackle the Egyptians, who were attempting to relieve pressure on Syria by launching a clumsy tank offensive.

Diplomacy

While Israel was shedding her illusions on the battlefield, the United States quickly devised a diplomatic strategy solidly based on a few illusions of her own. In the week preceding the war, Secretary of State Kissinger seems to have feared an Israeli pre-emptive strike in retaliation against the recent terrorist incident that had closed the Austrian way station for Soviet emigrants to Israel. [85] The Arab surprise attack did not alter Washington's conviction that Israel would win swiftly and devastate the Arab armies. To this assumption must be added a generous benefit of the doubt for Moscow. The night evacuation of embassy personnel on October 4, the lack of communication from Soviet leaders and the launching of a Soviet observation satellite [86] suggested foreknowledge and a violation of the consultation clauses in both the 1972 and 1973 documents of détente signed by Brezhnev and Nixon. But the Soviets did not appear to be pressing the conflict, and on the second day of war, it was reported already that Brezhnev had informed Nixon that the war should not interfere with détente. [87] Finally, the Saudi warnings of the previous summer concerning oil production suddenly assumed much more importance.

These three factors—the expected Israeli victory, the Soviet Union's apparent initial caution and the threat of oil embargo—shaped American policy during the first week of the war. Secretary of State Kissinger rapidly launched maneuvers designed to obtain a cease-fire, to protect détente if not to strengthen it, and to avoid giving cause for an oil embargo. Recognizing that the stalemate had been broken irrevocably by the fact of war, the United States sought to halt the hostilities as rapidly as possible but to do so in a fashion that facilitated movement toward a permanent settlement. [88] More specifically, Washington proposed joint U.S.-Soviet sponsorship of a cease-fire while avoiding any major gestures on Israel's behalf, especially on the question of arms supplies. The cease-fire proposal was expected to be most attractive to the Arabs as they neared defeat. The Soviets would cooperate to avoid a repetition of 1967. The Israelis could be constrained from ignoring such a cease-fire by their dependency on American political and military support. If the war could be concluded in this fashion, both Israel and the Arabs would fail to achieve their major battlefield aims, thereby creating conditions for negotiation; an oil embargo could be avoided for lack of a clear *casus belli* (such as a total Arab military defeat); and Soviet-American collaboration in crisis would be firmly established as a new factor in world politics.

Kissinger's policy depended on speedy agreement with the Soviet Union. In the meantime, cooperation from Moscow and the Arab oil producers would be jeopardized by very active American support of Israel. This boiled down rapidly to the question of American arms for Israel. While the U.S. government sought to gain Soviet help on a cease-fire resolution, the Israeli ambassador to Washington, Simha Dinitz, was shuffled between the White House and Defense Department. Ambassador Dinitz got the impression that Secretary of Defense James Schlesinger was dragging his feet. [89] The secretary of defense later claimed he could not have been dragging his feet because they were "clamped to the floor" by the White House. In view of Secretary Kissinger's general policy, it is hard to believe that he (or for that matter Schlesinger) favored strong help for Israel during the first week of the war. Given the expectation of Israeli victory, such assistance was both unnecessary and damaging to American diplomatic objectives. [90]

The whole operation bore all the classic marks distinguishing Kissinger's diplomatic method. He held the crucial cards; allies were to be manipulated as thoroughly as adversaries; rapid, consecutive movements were to coordinate war and diplomacy; and the Soviet-American conjunction would produce an amazing result when Moscow's immediate interest coincided with Washington's long-term benefit.

By October 13, however, the major assumptions of this policy had collapsed under the weight of events. The surprise and magnitude of the Egyptian-Syrian war effort cost the Israelis three days of confusion, heavy casualties, large numbers of tanks and planes and upset their order of battle. It was not going to be a short war, and the arms supply rapidly became critical to Israeli staying power. [91]

Equally important, Soviet policy had quickly emerged from what appeared to be initial passivity into full-fledged malignity. The question of Soviet foreknowledge of the war can be dealt with simply: all parties agree that Moscow knew the time of the Arab offensive at least two days in advance, and the Soviets have not denied the charge. The question of Soviet intentions, however, is another matter. Given the record of détente so frequently touted by the Nixon administration, the previous linkage between détente and Soviet behavior in the Middle East, and the absence of any overt Soviet intervention to affect the war in the first few days, Kissinger was loath to assume any deeper Soviet involvement. As he strove to produce a jointly sponsored cease-fire, he also publicly reminded Moscow of the principles of détente. On October 8, he declared:

We will oppose the attempt by any country to achieve a position of predominance either globally or regionally. We will resist any attempt to exploit a policy of détente to weaken our alliances. We will react if relaxation of tensions is used as a cover to exacerbate conflicts in international trouble spots. The Soviet Union cannot disregard these principles in any area of the world without imperiling its entire relationship with the United States.[92]

Later in the speech, Kissinger stated that "our policy with respect to détente is clear: We shall resist aggressive foreign policies. Détente cannot survive irresponsibility in any area, including the Middle East."[93] Within five days of this speech, the record was clearly established: Moscow opposed U.S. efforts for a cease-fire, urged other Arab states to enter the war, publicly advocated the use of the oil weapon against the West, and began a massive aerial resupply of the Egyptian and Syrian armies.[94] Still, according to Kissinger on October 12, this record, though not "helpful," was not irresponsible enough to threaten détente.[95] He was weighing "unhelpful" actions against the "relative restraint"—verbal restraint—supposedly shown by the Soviet media and Moscow's UN representatives. Kissinger refused to conclude that the Soviet Union knew of the war in advance; if she did, "we would consider it consistent and indeed required—by the principles that have been signed between the United States and the Soviet Union—that an opportunity be given to both sides to calm the situation."[96] These cautious statements are understandable in the context of strenuous U.S. efforts to reach a cease-fire agreement with Moscow before resupplying Israel. Kissinger's assessment of Soviet behavior up to October 12 was plainly that of the anxious diplomat rather than the careful historian: "If you compare their conduct in the crisis to their conduct in 1967, one has to say that Soviet behavior has been less provocative, less incendiary and less geared to military threats than in the previous crisis."[97]

American efforts were concluded on October 12 and 13, when Washington secured Jerusalem's agreement to a cease-fire-in-place; Moscow claimed that Cairo would accept the proposal if neither the United States nor the Soviet Union were its initial sponsor.

The British were asked for their good offices; Sadat was awakened at dawn to corroborate, and he denied the story.[98] If Sadat is to be believed, he also told the British ambassador of Soviet behavior that varied substantially from American hopes.[99] According to the Egyptian president, he and his ally, Assad of Syria, informed the Soviet ambassadors to their countries on Wednesday and Thursday, October 3 and 4, that Egypt and Syria were about to launch an offensive, with Assad stating the time. They also asked the Soviet government for its "attitude" toward the offensive. On Thursday, October 4, the Soviet ambassador to Egypt asked Sadat's permission to evacuate Soviet citizens by special arrangement. On Saturday, October 6, the ambassador brought word of his government's "attitude"; in Sadat's words, "the Soviet Union wanted a cease-fire after 48 hours," apparently implying that Syria agreed with this position. But Sadat emphasized that Egypt and Syria would not cease fire until their aims had been achieved. "The Soviet Ambassador was not satisfied," he said.

On Saturday evening, about six hours after the war had commenced, Sadat asserts that the Soviet ambassador told him the Syrians wanted a cease-fire; the Egyptian president then asked Assad to confirm this. The Syrian answer, which took nearly a day to send, was a denial, arriving shortly before the Soviet ambassador informed Sadat of a "second" Syrian cease-fire proposal. Sadat remonstrated angrily to the unlucky diplomat but also broached the subject of more Soviet tanks in view of the upcoming Egyptian offensive.

If these recollections are accurate, they present a worrisome picture. The Soviet government supported a short, limited campaign and risked its already shaky relationship with Sadat in trying to promote a cease-fire. Perhaps this was because Moscow believed the Israeli government's own overconfident announcements of impending military success. By October 10, however, the Israelis had admitted grave difficulties, the Americans had refrained from extensive arms shipments, and Washington had pressed anxiously for a cease-fire-in-place. The U.S.S.R. then embarked on a course designed to expand and prolong the war,

despite Kissinger's warnings on October 8. An Arab victory facilitated by a spectacular and efficient Soviet military airlift would
overcome Egyptian complaints and confirm Moscow's supremacy
in the Middle East. The détente linkage had been roughly cast
aside.

After the diplomatic reverse of October 13, Washington had
no choice but to respond. In Secretary Kissinger's own words, as
quoted by Marvin and Bernard Kalb, "We tried to talk in the first
week. When that didn't work, we said, fine, we'll start pouring in
equipment until we create a new reality." [100] The "new reality"
to be created, of course, was an impending Israeli victory. This
took approximately one week, from October 13 to October 20,
1973.

The Atlantic Partnership and the Oil Weapon

The American effort to create a "new reality" in the Middle
East soon encountered an old illusion: the Atlantic partnership.
The policies of most West European states toward the war were
dominated by fears of an oil embargo, whose economic consequences might doom their troubled governments already struggling with inflation and public dissatisfaction. Unlike previous
occasions, the United States had little to offer. In the European
view, American financial irresponsibility was a large contributor
to their inflation. The Western Hemisphere oil reserve and U.S.-
European sharing agreements, so useful in 1956 and 1967, no
longer existed. Furthermore, Washington had ignored the urgings
of Paris and, more recently, London that the Israelis had to be
made more "flexible" in order to displace a Soviet influence
feeding on the Middle East stalemate. Now the West Europeans
had to protect themselves from the consequences as best they
could.

When the war broke out, Western Europe and Japan possessed
temporary political and economic advantages over the United
States. The British, French and Japanese were demonstrably
pro-Arab or (as in Japan's case) "neutral" against Israel. Most

European states maintained oil reserves for sixty to ninety days of consumption; the Japanese had stocks for fifty-five days plus another twenty days en route. In contrast, the U.S. government did not know the extent of American oil inventories, possessed no machinery for collecting information beyond traditionally circumspect industry estimates and had already suffered spot shortages during the previous six months.[101]

The Arabs rapidly took advantage of U.S.-European differences in the hope of frustrating American political and military support for Israel. On October 17, eleven days after the beginning of the Yom Kippur War and three days after the commencement of the American airlift, ministers of eleven Arab states agreed to cut oil production and exports by 10 percent, with Saudi Arabia, Kuwait and Libya halting all oil shipments to the United States. In the pattern of its predecessors, the 1973 Arab oil embargo was launched to influence American policy after the American arms lift was described by Egypt as direct intervention.

The embargo drew strength from three factors. First, because of rising income from oil during 1971-1973, the Arab oil producers could finance the war effort and production restrictions simultaneously. Secondly, the Arab governments could enforce their dictate by threatening to seize the properties of companies refusing to honor the cuts without fear of retaliation. Finally, the United States, Western Europe and Japan lacked emergency sharing arrangements.

The Arab ministers realized that a 5 percent cut combined with a total embargo on the United States would damage Western Europe and Japan as well; they promised that anyone who supported the Arabs actively would "continue to receive the same oil supplies that they used prior to the reduction."[102] This statement was soon supplanted by an embargo against the Netherlands, ostensibly because of pro-Israeli statements by the Dutch government but more likely because Rotterdam was the main European oil port. All of these actions were designed to squeeze Washington by tightening American supplies and dividing the United States from her major allies.

The oil weapon—or, more correctly, European fear of the oil weapon—produced immediate dividends for the Arab cause in the form of a transatlantic quarrel over American policy and the resupply operation. The quarrel began with Britain. Initially, there was the still unexplained incident of the American request early in the war for a reconnaissance mission, using American aircraft, from Britain or Cyprus; the British agreed but wanted a "cover story," a detail that apparently angered the secretary of state, who canceled the mission and reportedly stopped intelligence reports to London.[103] Then came the cease-fire project and the incident with Sadat. Finally, once the American airlift was broached, London refused the use of an air base in Cyprus, citing its recently announced arms embargo, an embargo that affected Israel primarily, as the reason.

There was nothing to be asked of the French. The Pompidou government's attitude had been made plain enough through its earlier sale of Mirage jets to Libya and its stout refusal to be perturbed by their transfer to the Egyptian arsenal. The Spanish, Italian, Greek and Turkish governments refused landing and overflight rights. The West German authorities permitted arms shipments, until press reports of the loading of an Israeli ship forced Bonn to demand that its "strict neutrality" in the conflict be observed both in deed and word. Only Portugal cooperated fully, and her Azores air facilities served as the major refueling point for the American resupply operation.

The Alert: Détente and Dénouement

The oil embargo and the behavior of the West European states exploded the remaining American illusions about the oil threat and the Atlantic partnership. Both complicated but could not deflect the consequences of the American airlift or the renaissance of Israeli military fortunes. On October 14, Soviet Premier Kosygin tried again to talk Sadat into a cease-fire; two days later, the Egyptians lost a major tank battle involving more than 2,000 tanks. With the Israeli bridgehead across the Suez Canal expanding and his chief of staff physically broken, Sadat finally agreed to ask for a cease-fire on October 19.

The American strategy had not avoided the oil embargo or a major quarrel with the Europeans, but it could resume the pantomime of détente, thereby salvaging the main feature of the Nixon foreign policy. Everything depended on a cease-fire without an Egyptian defeat. In response to an urgent Soviet request, Kissinger hurried to Moscow on the weekend of October 19-21. The agreement that emerged deliberately adopted some of the details (cease-fire-in-place, opening of peace negotiations) advanced by the Israeli government in the more desperate days of the week before. As an additional persuasive measure, President Nixon asked the Congress on October 19 for $2.2 billion in aid to Israel. Secretary Kissinger then flew to Tel Aviv to persuade Premier Meir to accept the arrangement even though the tide had turned. On Sunday afternoon, October 22, 1973, both Egypt and Israel agreed to cease hostilities.

The secretary of state's timing was unfortunate. Within hours of the cease-fire, the Egyptians realized that the Third Army on the east side of the canal was nearly a hostage to the Israeli bridgehead behind them on the west side; they attempted to break out and Israel closed the ring. By Tuesday morning, October 24, the Egyptians were trapped, though they continued to fight in vain through the day. After learning of the Third Army's dilemma, Sadat appealed for U.S. and Soviet assistance to "maintain" the cease-fire; the United States refused. In Moscow, the Israeli advances could only be seen as a betrayal of the cease-fire deal, perhaps a double-cross by the Americans, and surely a dangerous threat to Soviet prestige. On October 24 Brezhnev wrote to President Nixon in a strong if not threatening manner, implying Soviet unilateral action. This impression was reinforced by Ambassador Dobrynin's representations to Kissinger and the sudden suspension of the Soviet airlift, ostensibly because the planes would be needed to transport Soviet paratroopers already on alert. [104]

The initial American response came on October 25, when the

United States announced a general Defcon-3 alert.[105] Later that day, the Soviets dropped their opposition to a UN resolution barring the major powers from participation in the proposed peacekeeping forces who were to monitor the shaky cease-fire. The Soviet arms airlift resumed. By the afternoon of October 26 the cease-fire began to take hold, and the atmosphere of an impending great-power collision eased.

The American alert soon became a subject of considerable controversy. Two important questions should have been asked. First, were American forces sufficient to deter a Soviet military intervention? Second, if a confrontation was threatening, what was left of détente?

The first question deals with American military credibility. Admiral Elmo Zumwalt, then chief of naval operations, has charged that American forces on the scene were inadequate: "Had we and the Russians clashed militarily in the Mideast their advanced state of military readiness would have given them a decided edge."[106] As a consequence, Zumwalt concluded, the United States was forced to accept Soviet terms and prevent Israel's destruction of the Egyptian Third Army. If Washington's conventional capacity could not prevent Soviet intervention, a nuclear threat—under conditions of U.S.-Soviet parity—hardly represented an option. After years of doubt over whether America would risk New York for Paris in a nuclear duel with the U.S.S.R., the idea of threatening nuclear war in behalf of Israeli military successes in Egypt was preposterous, especially when American policy was predicated on a cease-fire that denied overwhelming triumphs to either side.

If Soviet conventional advantages in the general context of U.S.-Soviet nuclear parity had indeed crippled American flexibility during the Yom Kippur War, the most ominous conclusions should have been drawn for Western Europe, where NATO had long faced superior Soviet forces. It implied a drastic decline in American ability to match Soviet military strength, with inevitable political deterioration to follow. Instead, the question of U.S. military credibility was submerged in the larger issue of presidential political credibility. As Kissinger had predicted in

May 1973, Watergate's erosion of the president's authority was indeed felt that autumn.

The secretary's timing, so unlucky thus far in the Middle East, now proved to be unlucky in Washington. While Kissinger was negotiating in Moscow, he had been surprised to receive authority to reach an agreement on cease-fire terms without reference to the White House. [107] The president was then suffering a major political disaster: the "Saturday night massacre," when Nixon fired Special Prosecutor Archibald Cox, compelling the resignations of Attorney General Elliot Richardson and his deputy, William Ruckelshaus, in the process. Coming on the heels of Vice President Agnew's resignation on October 10, after pleading nolo contendere to a charge of income tax evasion, the administration was now a shambles.

When he announced the alert to news reporters, the secretary of state found the president publicly suspected of creating a foreign military crisis to distract attention from his domestic problems. [108] Kissinger did not help Nixon's reputation when he revealed that the president had not attended the National Security Council meeting where it was decided to call the alert. [109] The secretary was finally forced to appeal for a "minimum of confidence" in the senior officials of the U.S. government. The alert had proved more credible in the Middle East than in Washington!

An equally serious difficulty turned on interpretations of the alert's political significance for détente. The desirable "minimum of confidence" was not bolstered by the Kissinger and Nixon accounts. In his October 25 news conference, the secretary of state stressed the "precautionary nature" of the alert and emphasized: "We do not now consider ourselves to be in a confrontation with the Soviet Union. . . . We are not talking of a missile crisis-type situation." [110] Challenged to describe the status of détente, he suddenly created a fresh balance sheet:

> If the Soviet Union and we can work cooperatively, first toward establishing a cease-fire, and then toward promoting a durable settlement in the Middle East, then the détente will have proved

itself. If this docs not happen, then we have made an effort—for which we have paid no price—that had to be made. And then one has to wait for another moment when the task of insuring or of bringing peace to mankind can be attempted.[111]

In a news conference the very next day, the president put a rather different construction on the event:

It was a real crisis. It was the most difficult crisis we have had since the Cuban confrontation of 1962. But because we had had an initiative with the Soviet Union, because I had a basis of communication with Mr. Brezhnev, we not only avoided a confrontation, but we moved a great step forward toward real peace in the Middle East.[112]

Later the president said that both the United States and the Soviet Union realized that Middle East differences should not be permitted to jeopardize "greater interests," such as arms control negotiations and European détente: "As a matter of fact, I would suggest that with all of the criticism of détente, that without détente, we might have had a major conflict in the Middle East. With détente, we avoided it."[113] Nixon concluded by reminding his audience that Brezhnev respected American power wielded firmly by a president who could withstand the harshest domestic criticism.

These statements revealed a powerful confusion. While the secretary played down the crisis to protect the main achievement of détente—lessening the risk of confrontation and nuclear war— the president played up the crisis to protect his reputation as a firm leader important to American national security. American power, even in its precautionary form, had brought the Soviets around; confrontation was not in their interest. Because of this "détente," a new opportunity for peace had been created. But the Nixon-Kissinger "structure of peace" could not disguise a relationship that corresponded precisely to the definition of détente attributed to a French journalist: "Détente is the Cold War waged by other means and sometimes the same means."

At the same time that the linkage between Soviet behavior in the Middle East and the intoxicating power of détente was being reaffirmed in Washington, the United States was moving rapidly to isolate the "greater interests" represented by détente from the Middle East crisis. The foundation for this maneuver was to be found in Secretary Kissinger's admission on October 25, 1973:

> The United States recognizes that the conditions that produced the war on October 6 cannot be permitted to continue, and the United States, both bilaterally and unilaterally, is prepared to lend its diplomatic weight to a serious effort in the negotiation process. [114]

Washington now understood that Sadat's war against the status quo, though it depended significantly on Soviet support, was in fact a bizarre gesture of confidence that only the United States could "deliver" Israel. Because the only substantial Soviet influence consisted of the arms supply, a process of negotiation moving toward settlement would perforce limit the Soviet role. Given the current circumstances of the Arab-Israeli dispute, Soviet policy was indeed difficult to reconcile with détente, as the war itself illustrated. But an American initiative, catering to Sadat's objectives without compromising Israeli security, would effectively "quarantine" both Soviet influence and potential damage to détente from another display of Moscow's misbehavior. If this could be done, Moscow would find itself with the weakest political position at the moment of its most effective military assistance to Cairo.

An American initiative was not long in coming, and it found Israel totally unprepared. The Israeli government did not grasp the change in the American position, that Washington would intervene to save Cairo. After the events of October 22-25, the final military dispositions left Israeli forces in control of the trapped Third Army's supply lines and in possession of important territory overlooking the Plain of Damascus. These potent bargaining tools were supplemented by the UN cease-fire text, Resolution 338, which prescribed immediate negotiations on the basis of Resolution 242. Bad memories of Washington's reluctance to supply arms during the first week, lack of information about Kissinger's trip to Moscow, and pressure to accept the cease-fire had been replaced by the gratifying airlift and alert.

Mrs. Meir was therefore astonished to receive an ultimatum from Secretary Kissinger early Saturday morning, October 27, that gave Israel the choice of allowing a resupply of the Egyptian Third Army or risking the loss of American support.[115] The Israelis decided to allow the resupply. Later, in the course of a Knesset debate, Moshe Dayan described the government's response: "We had no choice! Anyone who advocates the waging of a war in the context of a rift with the United States, advocates that we shall not be able to succeed in this war."[116] Premier Meir decided to go to Washington forthwith. Israel had run afoul of the Nixon administration's relationship with Moscow, threatening by her military actions to convert détente into confrontation.

The United Nations now proved its value as a resort for embarrassed governments. Egypt and Israel were both to save face through the insertion of a UN presence to conduct the relief operation, and troop separation became the main immediate issue. In the process, Israel thought she had gained a form of direct negotiation with Cairo and agreement to a peace conference in Geneva. These appeared to be major Egyptian concessions, which other Arab states would be bound to follow. But from the Egyptian point of view, the final trauma of the Third Army was bound to substantiate the long-held conviction of President Sadat and others that the United States, brought to reason by a show of Arab force, could be far more productive than Moscow in compelling Israeli concessions. The major Egyptian objective had been secured: the "status quo" was destroyed.

One final, nasty note marked the end of the war: the U.S.-European quarrel. The October 25 alert had been called by Washington with only perfunctory "consultation," and the Europeans disapproved. The next day, the Department of State censured the West European states for their lack of solidarity with U.S. policy; the secretary of defense promised "to [re-] consider established notions, established doctrines"; and the president concluded the critique by noting that "Europe, which gets

80 percent of its oil from the Mideast, would have frozen to death this winter unless there had been a settlement."[117] Chancellor Brandt of West Germany riposted on October 28, accusing the United States of neglecting consultation; in return, Kissinger vented his "disgust" with NATO.[118] In the aftermath of the war, Washington apparently found it easier to cooperate with its chief adversary than with its major allies.

3. OBSTACLES AND OPPORTUNITIES

The Recovery of American Foreign Policy:
The "Step-by-Step" Approach

The events of the Yom Kippur War nearly sank détente, disrupted the Atlantic Alliance and threatened economic disaster. The Arab and Soviet positions seemed strengthened enormously while Israel's outlook darkened. Nonetheless, the United States emerged from the war in a strangely advantageous position. The Nixon-Kissinger scheme of things had been shaken hard by October's events, but both the president and secretary of state were determined to reassert American authority and restore American prestige.

In the Middle East, the United States alone could negotiate with both Israel and the Arab states, and Egypt had launched the war with the primary aim of forcing American intervention. In relations with Western Europe and Japan, the United States also possessed advantages because she was less dependent on foreign sources of energy and better protected against the more dire effects of the financial crisis brewing for the oil consumers. In dealing with Moscow, Washington's hand was weaker, but important facets of détente such as the strategic arms talks and the European settlement symbolized by the Berlin Agreement still held.

American foreign policy as it emerged during 1974-1975 tied all of these factors together in a multipronged attempt to reverse or contain the damage to American interests wrought by the war. Washington's maneuvers were all the more remarkable in view of their political context: the decline and fall of Richard Nixon in the summer of 1974; his successor's inexperience at foreign policy; the Cyprus crisis, which weakened the U.S. position in the Eastern Mediterranean; the dramatic collapse of South Vietnam in the spring of 1975; and mounting criticism of Kissinger's policies.[119] The United States would attempt to fashion her flexibility in the Middle East and her advantages over her allies into a decisive renewal of American influence and Atlantic collaboration, thereby strengthening Washington's position against Moscow and the oil producers.

The new course set by Washington in the Middle East had been foreshadowed by the episode of the Egyptian Third Army. Soviet threats and the alert provided the drama, but American pressure on Israel effected the rescue. The litmus test of success for the leaders of Egypt, Syria and Jordan was Israeli withdrawal, and the United States alone could facilitate that without war. If Moscow's actions and objections undermined détente or Middle East peace, then these could be frustrated by U.S. diplomacy without confrontation. It fell to Kissinger to devise a mediation that would produce Israeli withdrawal without impairing Israeli security, all under American auspices.

The secretary of state's plan to achieve these formidable purposes turned out to be the "step-by-step" approach advocated by Assistant Secretary of State Sisco in the summer of 1973. This tactic was particularly well suited to the exhausted combatants because they could all make major tactical concessions without encountering strategic objections over territory or recognition. By June 1974 Kissinger successfully mediated disengagement agreements among Egypt, Israel and Syria. The UN forces constituted a buffer and warning signal between the opposing armies. The oil embargo was lifted after the first agreement, and the Egyptians reopened the Suez Canal in June 1975.

The American approach was not entirely successful in excluding certain issues, even during the first round of negotiations. The Geneva Peace Conference, under U.S. and Soviet cochairmanship, was intended to be the major vehicle for the "direct negotiations" Israel had long sought. Instead, both the United States and Israel lost interest in this forum shortly after the first Kissinger shuttle began in early 1974 to arrange Egyptian-Israeli disengagement. But the attempt to avoid Soviet obstruction at the peace conference encountered it instead on the Golan Heights. Unlike Egypt, Syria concluded the war without occupying any area taken by Israel in 1967. To improve its negotiating position, Damascus began a war of attrition during February 1974 that threatened to undo the Egyptian-Israeli agreement as well. After exhausting efforts, Kissinger was able to halt the conflict and Syria emerged—supported by Soviet arms—with a piece of the 1967 territory (Kuneitra). The Soviet Union had again demonstrated her usefulness in sustaining an Arab negotiating point.

The government of Golda Meir did not survive beyond the Syrian agreement. After months of struggle, Premier Meir was brought down by public outcry over the Agranat Commission's report on the war, which exonerated the politicians, particularly Defense Minister Dayan, and blamed the soldiers for the deficiencies exposed by the conflict. The premier, who had delayed her retirement in order to preserve peace in the party conflict over Dayan's demands, was undone in the end by the defense minister's loss of public support.

While the Labor Party nominee, Yitzchak Rabin (chief of staff in 1967 and later ambassador to Washington), tried to create a government, Kissinger accompanied President Nixon on his final foreign journey. Again the limits of the secretary's style and policy were exposed, this time by the Watergate reaction against wiretapping and secret maneuvers. The Congress voted confidence in Kissinger over wiretapping but was surprised to learn (as were the Israelis) of the nuclear reactor offer to Egypt and the financial assistance promised Syria.

The second round of step-by-step diplomacy took place under even stronger limitations. At Rabat, in September 1974, the Arab

states agreed on a "strait-jacket" principle: no individual settlements with Israel without complete withdrawal from all Arab
territories and satisfaction of Palestinian rights. Representation of
the latter was assigned to the Palestine Liberation Organization.
This threatened to deadlock everything because Israel would not
sit down with the PLO, and no Arab state could negotiate
substantial political concessions alone. But war was not an acceptable alternative for Washington, Cairo or Jerusalem, and the need
to avoid war soon produced the subterfuges necessary to take
another "step."

This time, the process ran afoul of Israeli politics. The events
of October had destroyed Israel's prewar confidence. She found
herself fighting under the handicaps of an isolated foreign policy
and a defective defense strategy, bringing intolerably high political and military casualties in their wake. Israel depended more
than ever on the United States, whose own position had been
seriously undermined by the war and which now sought to
reassert her influence by improving relations with the Arabs. If
Egyptian aims seemed more moderate, there remained the
troubling Palestinian question and the prospect of growing Arab
financial and political strength.

These elements were distilled by Premier Rabin into a single
problem: time.[120] Israel had to bargain her renewed military
strength and occupied territory for the time required by the
United States and her allies to reduce their energy dependency
and recover their political authority. This was a large vote of
confidence in Washington's own recovery plans and apparently
made room for considerable Israeli concessions in the step-by-step
process. But the tactical nuances of this strategy were understood
differently by the United States and Israel. Jerusalem now sought
refuge in Resolution 242's process of exchanging territory for
peace. The Rabin government offered a "piece of territory for a
piece of peace"; that is, an evacuation determined by the extent
that Arab political concessions changed the state of war toward a
"just and lasting peace."

In the spring of 1975, when Kissinger badly wanted a diplomatic triumph to offset the fall of Saigon, Israel tried to turn the

step-by-step process into a negotiation on the crucial issue of withdrawal/recognition. For Washington, this was both premature and unwise; a stalemate invited the Soviets to return, and a war was unacceptable. After a summer of extremely strained U.S.-Israeli relations, apparently seen by President Ford as a test of Executive authority in foreign policy, the Kissinger "mediation" was transformed into U.S.-Israeli, U.S.-Egyptian negotiations. What emerged in September 1975 was primarily an Egyptian commitment to extend the cease-fire; an Israeli withdrawal from militarily important Sinai passes and oil fields; a U.S. agreement to supply American "technicians" to operate an early-warning system as a token of Washington's political commitment; and extensive American political, financial and military pledges to both sides.

Whether this agreement lasts or another "step" is taken on the Syrian border, the United States had already begun to "guarantee" partial settlements, with the vital issues of the Palestinians, the quality of the peace and the Soviet role still untouched. The step-by-step tactic was approaching the strategic limits set by the Yom Kippur War when the military balance, Soviet intervention and the oil weapon would once again threaten American interests. The prolongation of the cease-fire through Israeli withdrawal, without losing Israeli confidence or involving the Soviet Union, had become increasingly difficult to achieve.

The Recovery of Atlantic Cooperation: The Energy Crisis

The pattern set by the step-by-step approach—initial and spectacular success without altering the strategic outlook—was duplicated in the effort to repair the Atlantic Alliance and resolve the energy problem. The Yom Kippur War did not kill the European Idea or suddenly rupture a healthy transatlantic relationship. It aggravated trends long evident. The West European states were suffering from individual impotence and collective frustration well before the October 1973 war, which simply threw their condition into high relief.

Impotence and frustration did not facilitate either European or transatlantic cooperation. There were essentially four routes for European action: cooperation with the United States and Japan outside of any institutional forum, the OECD, the EEC, and unilateral action.[121] Given their immediate supply situations, the embargo against the United States and Holland, and the obvious intention of the Arab oil producers to avoid offending their would-be supporters, the West European states were caught by conflicting policies. A mixture of unilateral behavior and European Community verbal unity triumphed. Despite the American remonstrations of late October 1973, which attempted to shock the Europeans into a realization of their own "best interests," the British and French continued to emphasize the "political protection" afforded by pro-Arab policies; they successfully opposed the OECD Oil Committee's activation of sharing plans on October 25 and 26, 1973.

When the Organization of Arab Petroleum-Exporting Countries (OAPEC) placed an embargo on oil exports to Holland and announced further production cuts to 75 percent of the September output, the Dutch demanded a pooling of oil resources under the Rome Treaty provisions. The French countered this by urging that the European Community adopt the French unilateral policy, which supported the Arab political position. On November 6 the Community called on Israel to "end the territorial occupation which it has maintained since the conflict of 1967." After this display of shared resolution, the European states were left to their own conservation measures, including speed limits, bans on Sunday driving, petroleum sales regulation and rationing plans. On November 18, the French policy apparently paid off when the OAPEC rewarded the West Europeans with a cancellation of the 5 percent cut planned for December. The United States and the Netherlands remained subject to the embargo.

The November EC resolution caught Kissinger in Cairo, trying to solidify the cease-fire and establish a negotiating process. He was offended and embarrassed. Now it was America's turn to complain about lack of consultation. What was worse, the European "strategy" proved to be particularly ineffective in preventing a reduction of crude-oil supply. France was the most dependent of the major European states on Arab oil (53 percent) and the United Kingdom the least (30 percent), with Germany in between (38 percent).[122] All three governments continued to apply more stringent measures to conserve fuel throughout November. Disputes in the British coal fields and French "solidarity" measures have been advanced as the main reasons for these restrictions, but the more important cause was to be found in the distribution mechanism: the international oil companies.

Bereft of government instructions, international sharing agreements or any political guidance, the American oil companies set the pace by deciding that they would comply with the embargo but not favor any customers. This commercial "sharing position" was designed to protect their sources in the Arab Middle East and their position in the United States from political reprisals.[123] By rerouting about 30 percent of their shipments, the American companies juggled a 19 percent cutback in Arab production (a total of 4 million barrels per day at its height), an increase in production of 1 to 1.5 million barrels daily by non-Arab producers, and a complete embargo on the United States so that the overall reduction of crude oil and petroleum products exported to the United States, Europe and Japan was held to less than 18 percent of prewar deliveries.[124] In the course of this operation, the oil companies were obstructed not only by ambiguous Arab categories ("most favored," "preferred," "neutral") but by export restrictions and stockpiling regulations imposed by individual European states.[125] As a consequence of company action, however, expectations in Paris and London that Western Europe would be spared reductions proved to be illusory.

The relationship between the embargo and OPEC's prices was also misunderstood. Some of this could be laid to the coincidence of dates. On October 16, 1973, the day before the embargo, the Persian Gulf oil producers, accounting for half the oil exports to noncommunist countries, abolished the Teheran Agreement and increased the posted price by 17 percent while raising oil company taxes. Higher prices were soon declared by all OPEC members. It could be argued that the embargo was the main force driving prices up; if the embargo were removed, the price would decline.

The main problem with this thesis is that the embargo's strength derived more from OPEC's growing power to set prices and production than the reverse. Until this became clear, the unilateral pro-Arab policies advocated by Paris and London dominated the European approach. Kissinger's call in early December for a great joint effort by the United States and her principal allies to devise short- and long-term policies to meet the energy crisis, got a cold reception at the EC summit in Copenhagen. Meeting on December 14 and 15, the European Community reaffirmed its November 6 Middle East declaration, called for the development of a European common energy market proposal and asked for more OECD studies. The heart of the meeting, however, was the Dutch demand for energy sharing and the French proposal for closer European-Arab ties, emphasized by the unexpected appearance of several Arab foreign ministers. The Dutch were put off once again, the French proposal was embodied in the final communiqué, and the Danish foreign minister had to tell the Arab "guests" that the oil squeeze was no longer productive, despite the French and British positions.

Even as the European Community met, its policy had become irrelevant to the real oil squeeze. "Squeeze" was a misnomer if it referred to a physical shortage; the Europeans were easily tided over the crisis by their extensive reserves, even with the 18 percent reduction in crude and product.[126] The embargo, the panic to buy oil at any price and the lack of consumer cooperation simply sharpened OPEC's already formidable power to determine prices, demonstrated over the previous eighteen months. (The posted price had been more than doubled between January 1972 and October 16, 1973.)[127] On December 11, more than 80 million barrels of Iranian crude oil (government owned) were auctioned to U.S., European and Japanese firms at $14 to $17 a barrel. In a striking demonstration of their new authority, the Persian Gulf states announced shortly thereafter in Teheran that the posted price would more than double (from $5.11 to $11.65) on January 1, 1974. This edict was unaffected by the restoration of production cuts (but not the end of the embargo) projected by OAPEC two days later as a reward for the Copenhagen summit. Supplies would thus be increased simultaneously with price, a convincing demonstration of monopoly power.

Damaged though they were by conflicting interests, the bonds of Atlantic cooperation were not entirely withered. The new danger posed by the stupendous cost of imported oil temporarily submerged all transatlantic conflicts over trade and payments deficits. Just as Western Europe could not hope to defend itself against Soviet pressure without American support, so the Europeans now could not hope to negotiate successfully their economic perils without Washington's cooperation. American strategy sought to take advantage of this residual common interest and Washington's more favorable energy situation.[128] President Nixon re-emphasized the need for national self-sufficiency in Project Independence, announced November 7, 1973, and various adminstrative measures, including price control and petroleum allocation were introduced. This was followed by Kissinger's call for international cooperation in December and the president's invitations to a Washington Energy Conference of the major countries for February 1974.[129]

The European Community countries now found themselves moving toward the perilous choice of cooperation with Washington or an "independent" European stance along the lines of French policy. The reality of the energy situation was still not reflected in the EC meetings at Brussels on February 5, where the ministers concentrated on limiting the scope of the Washington Energy Conference: "The Washington Conference . . . should not serve to institutionalize a new framework of international cooperation." [130] Instead, the EC emphasized a potential special regional relationship between Europe and the Middle East, a relationship given more specific form by rumors of large, impending barter deals exchanging French industrial goods and arms for long-term supplies at good prices.

In the event, matters were reversed: the French barter deals proved to be false rumors or small scale, and the other European states agreed at the conference to the establishment of a new framework for international cooperation. Despite French objections and attempts to depict a fundamental divergence in U.S.-European interests, the United States was plainly in the best economic position, enjoyed important political relationships with Iran, Saudi Arabia and Venezuela, and wielded the most effective diplomacy in the Arab-Israeli dispute. For Western Europe to strike out independently of Washington suddenly seemed silly. Though Paris refused to accept all aspects of the final communiqué, the other Europeans and the Japanese agreed to develop a comprehensive energy program, to coordinate financial measures, to establish a senior coordinating group and to plan a consumer-producer conference.

The Energy Coordinating Group established by the Washington conference eventually developed an agreement for a cooperative program, which was signed in Paris on November 15, 1974; it created an International Energy Agency (IEA) under the OECD, with sixteen participating countries. The IEA's major tasks were to develop

(1) a common level of emergency self-sufficiency in oil supplies, "including restraint measures and emergency allocation";

(2) an information system covering the international oil market;

(3) a long term cooperation program in order to reduce dependence on imported oil; and

(4) cooperative relations with oil producers and other oil consumers.

Currently, the IEA provides for a "self-sufficiency" target of sixty days (to be raised to ninety days over the next few years), counting stocks, standby production facilities and emergency allocation. The trigger for emergency sharing is a 7 percent reduction in supplies. The allocation procedure is also linked to the type and extent of embargo and requires consumption restraint as well. In addition, by May 31, 1975, the Kissinger-Simon "safety net" was established under the OECD, consisting of a potential $25 billion in national commitments or guarantees (according to a formula derived from GNP and foreign trade). As a "last resort," a country suffering crippling payments deficits owing to oil imports can obtain relief provided particularly that it measures up to the OECD Financial Support Fund's policies and objectives. (Norway became a nonvoting "associate member" of the IEA and a full member of the "safety net"; France established an "informal" liaison with the IEA and became a full member of the "safety net.") These developments have also been accompanied by a special IMF oil fund of $3.5 billion and an EC fund of $3 billion.

Such signs of Atlantic cooperation were a welcome relief from the suspicions and quarrels of 1973. These signs were also accompanied by political changes. The governments in London, Paris and Bonn feared correctly that their inability to influence events affecting their troubled economies would endanger them electorally. But Heath, Pompidou and Brandt laid hold of the wrong measures to protect themselves—political statements and actions that provoked a quarrel with Washington in order to protect against an embargo—when their reserve supplies easily tided them over the crisis, and the distribution system apportioning the crude-oil shortage was not in their hands. Within six months after the war, they were all out of office, in each case replaced by men with much less faith in the puny business of dealing with the oil producers alone.

The revival of allied cooperation could not disguise serious problems. Secretary Kissinger had identified these at the Washington Energy Conference: the political issue of the manipulation of raw materials to dictate foreign policies and the economic issue of high oil prices. "Current price levels," he said, "are simply not sustainable."[131] But the market strategy adopted by the consumers—conservation, alternative sources and political pressure— has not lowered OPEC's price. Seventy-seven percent of Japan's energy is still supplied by imported oil, and the European Community draws 60 percent from foreign sources (42 percent from OAPEC); 17 percent of U.S. energy is now imported, and 4 percent comes from Arab sources.[132] Furthermore, the drop in oil consumption throughout the industrial world during the past year is probably due less to official conservation than to the prevailing economic recession.[133]

Prospects for alleviating this situation seem poor as national energy planners encounter the limits imposed by geography and money. In a report on Project Independence—designed above all to exploit U.S. resources, put pressure on OPEC and ease Atlantic dependence on imports—the U.S. Federal Energy Administration concluded on the sour note that energy supplies, especially petroleum, could not be greatly increased during the next four years; U.S. reserves may not be very large in any event.[134] Moreover, the international oil price plays a major role in determining the future cost—and supply—of all energy sources, a prospect that seemingly offers OPEC the choice of maximizing price until alternatives are developed to petroleum, then minimizing price to foreclose them. The strategies for decreasing import vulnerability all seemed to involve extraordinary investment, continuing high prices, significant government intervention into energy markets, massive environmental problems and major social change.

The political nature of the energy problem is also persistent and serious. OPEC, prodded energetically by Algeria, has sought to depict efforts to disrupt it as an industrial-country design to sustain an unfair international economic order. The first Consumer-Producer Conference, held in Paris during December 1975, reached uneasy compromises between the U.S. position that discussion should focus on high petroleum prices and the attempt by OPEC and others to broaden the subject to larger economic issues such as inflation, indexation of commodities with industrial products and "mandatory" foreign assistance. Meanwhile, numerous "commodity" associations are hoping to duplicate OPEC's success. But the position of the industrial states has improved, largely because high oil prices have burdened the less developed consuming countries with balance-of-payments emergencies.[135]

Thus, two years after the war, the United States had succeeded in restoring Atlantic collaboration on a series of emergency measures to deal with a potential embargo and financial problems arising from imported-oil bills. But this strategy has not dealt effectively with OPEC's power to set prices, and it does not begin to deal with the issue of Atlantic cooperation against the demands of the less developed countries. The reassertion of American leadership has stabilized the Atlantic Alliance temporarily without dealing with the long-term problems of its relationship to the rest of the world.

The Future of Détente

Washington's remarkable assertion of influence in the Middle East and the recovery of minimal alliance cohesion on the energy problem overshadowed momentarily the main strategic problem facing the United States after the October 1973 war: the relationship with the Soviet Union. Despite the best efforts of the president and secretary of state, détente had been badly damaged.

In the spring of 1975, even Kissinger admitted that détente was stagnating.[136] Nixon's last summit meeting had been barren of results; the trade agreement had been rejected by Moscow after complicated negotiations concerning the relationship of American economic policy to Soviet emigration practices. The Vladivostok Agreement on strategic arms, which emerged from the first Ford-Brezhnev meeting, faced significant obstacles. The collapse of South Vietnam, developments in Portugal, the Helsinki summit and the Angolan civil war had all stimulated a growing criticism of détente. These events and the Soviet role in the Yom Kippur War were interpreted by Kissinger's critics to indicate a pattern of Soviet deception and bad faith, while the United States continued to rely recklessly on Moscow's unkept promises.[137]

Détente runs to the heart of American foreign policy, and its defense has become a major project of President Ford and Secretary Kissinger. In their view, more restrained behavior by the United States and the Soviet Union is essential if the world is to survive the nuclear age. Because of a growing "interdependence," Moscow and Washington must also take the lead in promoting cooperation to resolve universal problems. Détente is not a static state of affairs but simply the "process" of establishing such understanding and cooperation. Détente can progress or regress. It requires vigilant American participation internationally to ensure an outcome favorable to American values.

These propositions are not generally contestable. Indeed, Kissinger's own public description of Soviet foreign policy to the Senate Foreign Relations Committee certainly portrays a hostile though cautious adversary very much in the tradition of his sterner critics.[138] The argument over détente, particularly where it concerns the Middle East, has more to do with three questions. Do the Soviets have an equal stake with the United States in restraining regional situations from developing into potential confrontation? If so, does this stake commit them to cooperation with the United States in resolving regional conflict? Finally, will this cooperation persist even if Soviet regional influence diminishes?

Before the Yom Kippur War, hopes for détente were based on the notion that the answer to all three questions was yes. But more than any other recent event, the war revealed Moscow's ability to exploit regional problems while simultaneously affirming its desire to avoid confrontation. The defenders of détente therefore have been forced to place decidedly odd interpretations on Soviet behavior during October 1973 in order to sustain the necessary assumptions about Moscow's stake in moderation. Secretary Kissinger, for example, has projected a picture of Soviet restraint—indeed bewilderment—over events in the Middle East, suggesting also that Moscow's behavior was less malevolent and less important than generally presumed. Testifying to a congressional committee on September 19, 1974, the secretary said:

> It gives the Soviets too much credit to believe that they can unleash a Middle East crisis by themselves. . . . I do not believe that they wanted a war in 1973. What I believe happened was that in an ongoing relationship with Arab countries, they were not prepared to give up that relationship, and so everybody last year slid into a situation that was unforeseen and not sufficiently controlled.[139]

Before the Senate Finance Committee on December 3, 1974, however, Kissinger admitted that the Soviet Union had violated some principles of understanding with the United States during the Yom Kippur War:

> Of course, I would say basically that when the Soviet Union urges other countries to participate in a war any place, that it would be violating the basic principles of the 1972 agreement. Now then, one has to analyze why the Soviet Union may have done this.[140]

These statements and others like them were part of the administration's anxious and somewhat confusing redefinition of the détente relationship during 1974-1975 to accommodate the impact of the Middle East war. The 1972-1973 Brezhnev-Nixon principles were not the solemn obligations popularly supposed when they were signed but "an aspiration and a yardstick by which we assess Soviet behavior.[141] More importantly, the process of détente had to be assessed by "levels." Détente had progressed on three of these levels: arms control, bilateral contacts and relaxation of tensions in areas of direct superpower concern (such as Berlin). But on the fourth level, areas "peripheral" to the vital interests of the superpowers (such as the Middle East), progress was distinctly uneven. At the same time, Ford and Kissinger have inveighed against "selective détente" and warned that the United States will not be prevented, in Ford's words, "from going in and meeting the challenges where the Soviet Union is involved."[142]

Such ambiguous, if not contradictory, concepts and the "nuances" of the administration's defense of détente undoubtedly are designed to leave the opposition only fleeting shadows to attack, even at the cost of clarity. But U.S. policy since the Yom Kippur War has plainly sought a series of priorities, which turn out to be the three "levels" where progress can be made with the Soviets. Where progress cannot be made, such as the Middle East, precautions must be taken using both American military power and diplomacy to ensure that conflict does not jeopardize other achievements. In other words, instead of linking Soviet behavior in the Middle East to the process of détente, the process of détente must be protected against the dangers of Soviet behavior in the Middle East.

The selective or hierarchical notion of détente pursued by the United States is based on the experience of the Yom Kippur War and an appreciation of the Soviet position in the region. Moscow made clear during October 1973 not only its capacity to exploit strategic opportunities but its willingness to run the risk of confrontation in a peripheral area. But these strong demonstrations disguised an essentially weak political position. Unable to attract adherents through ideology or economic assistance, the Soviet Union's only effective source of influence is in arms supply and military deterrence. These are unstable instruments, giving the U.S.S.R. a role in making war but little incentive to establish peace—unless that peace would also establish a stable Soviet influence. The Soviet Union's great power to encourage violence and her small incentive and responsibility to encourage peace discredit Moscow as a mediator among the local parties. Soviet persistence in trying to alter the local balance of power and somehow confirm her equality, if not supremacy, in the region, even at the cost of irritating Washington and endangering vital American interests, is obviously imcompatible with détente. As Kissinger put it, "Should it [the Soviet government] seek to use détente as a device for selective exploitation of strategic opportunities, the entire fabric of our evolving relationship will be brought into question."[143]

The American step-by-step diplomacy and Kissinger's awkward attempts to explain away Moscow's behavior during October 1973 were intended in part to delay the impact of selective exploitation on the "entire fabric." But the essentially tactical nature of the step-by-step procedure, though effectively playing down the Soviet role, has begun to encounter its strategic limits in relationship to Moscow as well as to the local parties. The U.S.S.R. has given ample proof that she will not be deterred by quarrels with particular Arab states or by Kissinger's ingenuity from pursuing her local interests, even if this encourages the more violent parties to the Arab-Israeli dispute. The future of détente is therefore bound up to an extraordinary degree with Soviet behavior in the Middle East.

The Yom Kippur War: End of Illusion?

The implications of the Yom Kippur War for American foreign policy can be appreciated by comparing the distribution of international power before and after the war. Before October 1973 the United States could argue that the world was moving toward a multipolar "structure" of peace, sustained by great-power restraint and even collaboration through the process of Soviet-American détente. Given the economic strength of Western Europe and Japan and the new connection with China, the United States could cut her military commitments without endangering her interests. Washington would substitute diplomacy and economic advantage for the military might and political will to employ force that the Vietnam misadventure had discredited. By linking the progress of détente to the amelioration of regional issues, by emphasizing that détente would not prevent the United States from contesting regional challenges, the United States hoped that great-power restraint would contain regional conflict.

This perception of the world was exploded by the war. Three weeks of violence in the Middle East sufficed to raise fundamental questions concerning the stability and validity of the new Soviet-American relationship, the survival of the Atlantic Alliance and the actual "power" of Western Europe and Japan. Détente nearly died of confrontation; the hasty reassertion of American leadership drew allied protests; and the Europeans and Japanese proved unable to influence the outcome of events. The new centers of power proclaimed by the Nixon Doctrine looked more like new centers of weakness, for their impressive economic power required energy whose sources they did not control.

An even greater change in perception of power came from the Middle East. Sadat later boasted that his persistent refusal to agree to a cease-fire enabled the Arabs to launch an embargo, making them the "sixth world power."[144] Exaggeration notwithstanding, the power of OPEC rather than the Arab embargo was now confirmed as a new factor in international politics. The "sixth power," however, was created by a redistribution of economic and political strength from the industrial to the nonindustrial states; it is not a new power based on national military or technological capacities. This redistribution was at the expense of the United States and her allies, whose political and economic strength in relation to the rest of the world had plainly declined. Relations between the principal industrial states and the less developed countries, which formerly consisted of foreign aid and trade concessions within an international economic system dominated by Atlantic preferences, now had to be placed on a different footing. This change was greatly accelerated through the indirect economic consequences of the war, represented by OPEC's December 1973 price increases. Its effects are not yet completely clear. The ideological alliance of the nonindustrial oil producers and oil importers against the industrial states may not withstand the pressure imposed by the oil price long enough for the "redistribution" to save the more fragile economies.

The events of October 1973 also lent substance to Moscow's claims of equal status with Washington. The war confirmed the Soviets' ability to exploit regional problems to their own advantage. Besides her handsome killing on the international oil market,[145] the Soviet Union gained new prestige from her military prowess as analysts hastened to dissect the significance of portable anti-tank weapons and the SAM systems. Perhaps most importantly, Soviet capacity to intervene with air and naval forces beyond continental Europe had grown to impressive proportions. The October war demonstrated once again the industrial basis of modern arms, the importance of having *enough* weapons, where a quantitative superiority can be translated into a qualitative advantage on the battlefield. An American study concluded:

> What the Soviets gave the Arabs was not sophistication, but proliferation. It was the vast number of weapons provided the Arabs rather than any exceptional technical capability that took a toll. It is important to ask ourselves . . . at what point does a great advantage in quantity overcome an advantage in quality?[146]

The respective American and Soviet supply operations brought to light serious weaknesses in the American logistics base for tanks and certain weapons categories.[147] In a larger sense, the war thus confirmed a trend in an area détente has not been able to alter: Soviet priorities. Moscow's emphasis on the instruments of power, despite a seriously troubled economy, had produced an efficient and large-scale military establishment with global capacities. The Atlantic Alliance, in contrast, possessed a steadily shrinking military establishment despite the economic boom that lasted until the early 1970s.

The shift in the distribution of power affected Israel most of all. The Yom Kippur War transformed Israel from an important, semi-independent American ally into a controversial, dependent American client. The Jewish State emerged militarily victorious at an enormous cost, more dependent on a single outside state than at any time since 1948 and virtually isolated from the major international political groupings. As a heavy importer of finished goods, and lacking energy resources outside of captured Egyptian oil fields, Israel fell into the category of those states most adversely affected by the price of oil. Protected temporarily from this disaster through American largess and the Abu Rodeis oil fields, Israel had no hope of joining the alliance of the less developed and scant welcome from most of the Europeans and the Japanese.

Important ambiguities remained in the Arab position on peace, such as Palestinian rights, which eroded the satisfaction of beginning negotiations "without preconditions." The more modest Arab goals were in any event to be sustained by much greater financial and political strength, which might negate Israeli military advantages as it did from October 24 to 29. Worst of all, the Israelis were bound closer than ever to the United States at a moment when the American international position had weakened and Washington's interest in improving relations with the Arabs had assumed urgent necessity.

These changes in the distribution and perception of power were not the only implications for American foreign policy. The

Yom Kippur War made the success or failure of Washington's Middle East maneuvers a crucial determinant of the entire American international position.

Because détente, the Atlantic Alliance and the energy problem are still subject to inordinate disturbance by the Arab-Israeli dispute, the United States has committed herself to produce a quick settlement of the conflict. This will require an arrangement satisfying all the major contestants on the subjects of Israeli withdrawal, Arab recognition and Palestinian rights, leaving no party unhappy enough to seek Soviet help in the hope of bettering its position. It is easy to foresee that the United States will not be able to fulfill Arab expectations without shaking Israeli confidence. It is difficult to foresee how international or even unilateral American guarantees can overcome the problem of assuring Israeli security in the pre-1967 war boundaries. Failure to achieve such a settlement, however, would lay the basis for a renewel of Soviet influence through an arms supply and a persistent danger to American political and economic interests. An American "solution" is necessary; indeed, it is demanded by the principal Arab states and Israel. Whether it can be achieved despite Moscow and the bitterness of the dispute remains to be seen.

Meanwhile, an American policy to deal with the essential issues of a less favorable distribution of power and a lasting Arab-Israeli settlement still lacks formulation. Two years after the Yom Kippur War burst Israeli and American illusions about Egyptian strategy, détente, the Atlantic Alliance and the oil weapon, the principal victims, led by the United States, have stabilized their positions but not necessarily improved their long-term prospects. Utilizing a series of tactical advantages over the Soviet Union in the Middle East, over her allies on the energy problem, over Israel through that state's isolated dependency, America has prolonged the cease-fire, promoted emergency measures against economic catastrophe and preserved a semblance of détente.

But this virtuoso performance does not fundamentally resolve any of the strategic problems facing the United States in trying to balance Soviet power, revive the Atlantic Alliance and alleviate the energy problem. Despite temporary achievements, the flow and perception of power remain the same. Moreover, an end to Washington's tactical mobility can already be foreseen, when avoidance of divergent interests and the hard facts of Soviet strength will no longer be possible. Some of the global implications are already evident. The People's Republic of China, whose own security is heavily involved with the success or failure of the Western democracies, has become an ardent advocate of European unity and a caustic critic of Soviet-American détente. Washington's relationship with Peking is also nearing the point where it will be drained of strategic potential unless the United States and her allies strengthen their positions against the Soviet Union or collaborate more extensively with the Chinese in anti-Soviet policy.[148]

These difficult conditions emphasize one final illusion still besetting the United States. Since 1969 the Nixon Doctrine and other formulations have been employed to convince the American people and the world that U.S. interests can still be sustained despite a smaller U.S. effort, a less potent military posture and a reduced international commitment. The 1969-1973 "transition period," from the old bipolarity to the new multipolarity, supposedly registered the efficient execution of this change without substantial loss of American prestige or power.

The Yom Kippur War and its consequences demonstrated that this too was a false hope. The emergency energy-sharing and financial arrangements promoted by Washington in 1974-1975, though far from resolving the long-term issues, have already placed additional burdens on the United States. It is obvious that further protection of American interests will require more obligations, not less; greater risks of military involvement; and a sustained consensus on the purposes and means of American activity abroad. That this occurs in the context of reduced American authority does not make these elements less necessary. The Yom Kippur War thus initiated a series of developments that threaten to collide dramatically with American reluctance to assume new international responsibilities.

It is indeed true that "almost all our misfortunes in life come from the wrong notions we have about the things that happen to us. To know men thoroughly, to judge events sanely is, therefore, a great step towards happiness."[149] The surprise and magnitude of the Yom Kippur War demonstrated that Washington's notions about what was happening in the world were wrong. American foreign policy grossly mistook the real distribution of power, overrated the restraining force of détente and exaggerated the strength of U.S. allies. The diffusion of power from the Atlantic countries could not be controlled by the economic "strength" of the European Community, the "principles of coexistence" or the "structure of peace." Multipolarity could not protect the West from political mishap, and "interdependence" with the oil producers did not necessarily strengthen Western civilization.

A "great step towards happiness" now requires a more sober American estimate of the value of détente, the condition of the Atlantic Alliance and the industrial world's energy position, all of which are influenced by the Arab-Israeli dispute. U.S. efforts to remedy the dispute, even at the cost of additional commitments, will demonstrate whether American leaders have rescued "sane judgment" from the illusions that preceded the Yom Kippur War.

NOTES AND REFERENCES

1. See Bernard Lewis, The Middle East and the West. New York: Harper & Row (1964). Also see Albert Hourani, Arab Thought in the Liberal Age: 1798-1939. London: Oxford Univ. Press (1967). Arab political thought can be divided into Islamic fundamentalism or versions of European ideologies.

2. See Harold W. Glidden, "The Arab world," Amer. J. of Psychiatry (February 1972), pp. 984-988.

3. See Michael Brecher, The Foreign Policy System of Israel. New Haven: Yale Univ. Press (1972); esp. part 2, "Psychological environments," pp. 211-318.

4. For a fuller description of Israel's military doctrine, see Michael Handel, Israel's Political-Military Doctrine. Cambridge: Harvard Univ. Center for Internatl. Affairs, Occasional Paper in Internatl. Affairs No. 30 (July 1973).

5. This was especially true of Nasser's Pan-Arabism. For a recent Egyptian statement seeking to allay such suspicions by contrasting Nasser's tendency to engage in "peripheral battles" with Sadat's concentration on the "main battle," see "Statement of Abdul Al-Quddus (chairman of Al-Ahram) on relations with Arab countries, USSR," Foreign Broadcast Information Service: Middle East and North Africa, hereafter cited as FBIS (October 6, 1975), p. D7.

6. Arnold Krammer, The Forgotten Friendship. Urbana: Univ. of Illinois Press (1974).

7. Oles M. Smolansky, The Soviet Union and Arab East Under Khrushchev. Lewisburg: Bucknell Univ. Press (1974). Moscow never ceased to hope that Arab "socialism" would redound to Soviet benefit, but when a choice arose between supporting local communist parties or governments whose foreign policies abetted Soviet interests, the latter were always preferred, even if this meant disaster for the local communists.

8. Charles Yost, "How it began," Foreign Affairs (January 1968), pp. 308-311. See also Mohammed Heikal, Nasser: The Cairo Documents. London: New English Library (1972), p. 217.

9. Lyndon Baines Johnson, From the Vantage Point: Perspectives of the Presidency. New York: Popular Library (1971), pp. 301-303.

10. More than 200 aircraft were supposedly delivered within a few weeks; by October, 80 percent of Egypt's losses had been replaced. See Lawrence L. Whetten, The Canal War: Four Power Conflict in the Middle East. Cambridge: Unit Press (1974), p. 59.

11. See Arthur Lall, The UN and the Middle East Crisis, 1967. New York: Columbia Univ. Press (1968), pp. 206-207, 211-212.

12. Shabtai Teveth, Moshe Dayan. Jerusalem: Weidenfeld & Nicholson (1972), pp. 333-334. The Soviets were shipping heavy military supplies to North Vietnam through the Suez Canal.

13. William B. Quandt, Fuad Jabber and Ann Mosely Lesch, The Politics of Palestinian Nationalism. Berkeley: Univ. of California Press (1973), pp. 94-113.

14. See "Summary of resolution of Arab summit conference, Khartoum, Sudan, September 1, 1967," in John Norton Moore [ed.], The Arab-Israeli Conflict. Princeton: Princeton Univ. Press (1974), Vol. 3, p. 788. The Arab oil-producing states also dropped their embargo and offered about $378 million quarterly to Egypt and Jordan as a war subsidy.

15. See Gideon Rafael, "UN Resolution 242: a common denominator," New Middle East (June 1973). See also Lall, p. 124 et passim.

16. Dayan's inclusion in the cabinet on June 5 was called "a minor putsch" by Premier Levi Eshkol. See Terence Prittie, Eshkol: The Man and the Nation. New York: Pitman (1969). Golda Meir was also known to have strenuously opposed the inclusion of the opposition in a national unity government.

17. Whetten, p. 61.

18. See Dayan's statement in the New York Times (January 29, 1970) and the interview with Golda Meir, New York Times (February 8, 1970).

19. New York Times (February 8, 1970).

20. A Lasting Peace in the Middle East: An American View, speech of Secretary of State William P. Rogers before the Galaxy Conference on Adult Education on December 9, 1969. Washington: GPO (1970). A U.S. plan for an Israeli-Jordanian settlement was revealed on December 22, 1969, by the New York Times. It followed the principles set forth in the Rogers speech. For Israeli reactions, see Policy Background: An Analysis of the U.S. Mideast Peace Plan (December 24, 1969); available from the Israeli Embassy, Washington. Also see Golda Meir's Knesset statement of December 29, 1969, in the Jerusalem Post (weekly overseas ed., December 30, 1969). The Soviet Union also rejected the plan; see the New York Times (January 13, 1974).

21. Presidential Advisor on National Security Affairs Henry Kissinger spoke of "expelling" the Soviets from Egypt on June 26; on July 1, President Nixon remarked that Israel was entitled to "defensible" not just "secure" borders. New York Times (June 27 and July 2, 1970).

22. Nixon's commitments included a willingness to consider a permanent military and political relationship with Israel after a peace treaty. See Michael Brecher, Decisions in Israel's Foreign Policy. New Haven: Yale Univ. Press (1975), pp. 491-495. The government's original rejection of the Rogers proposal was considered so insulting by Ambassador Rabin that he refused to deliver it until it was toned down.

23. Israel's vulnerability to the missiles had been demonstrated in early July when eight SAM batteries on the southern sector of the Suez Canal (well away from the main front) were destroyed; the Israeli Air

Force lost five F-4s and two A-4s in the process. Israel exacted her revenge on July 30, 1970, by destroying four Soviet-manned MiGs in deliberately provoked aerial combat. Perhaps in response, the missile movement into the "standstill zone" commenced on August 2, five days before the cease-fire, indicating Moscow's decision to strengthen ground defenses rather than increase aircraft commitments.

24. The United States temporized for more than three weeks before acknowledging on September 1 that violations had occurred; there were then forty-five SAM sites in the "standstill zone," including Egyptian-manned SAM-2s and Soviet-manned SAM-3s. The Israeli government, under the threat of Dayan's resignation, refused to enter negotiations unless new American arms were forthcoming. When Washington complied, Cairo charged the United States with betraying her commitment not to arm Israel further during the cease-fire period.

25. Marvin Kalb and Bernard Kalb, Kissinger. Boston: Little, Brown (1974), pp. 196-209.

26. Moore, Vol. 3, p. 1,104.

27. The American, British and French governments greeted the Egyptian reply with a surprising burst of enthusiasm, given the vagueness of the language. So did the columnists. See, for example, James Reston, "The coming U.S.-Israeli crisis," New York Times (March 4, 1971).

28. New York Times (May 14, 1971). The African attitude may be found in West Africa (October 15, 1973) and in Susan Aurelia Gitelson, Israel's African Setback in Perspective. Jerusalem: Hebrew Univ., Leonard Davis Instit. for Internatl. Relations, Jerusalem Paper on Peace Problems No. 6 (May 1974).

29. The proposal, originated by Israeli Defense Minister Moshe Dayan, also featured a "separation of forces" aspect, but without Egyptian forces on the east side of the Suez Canal. See Whetten, pp. 67-71.

30. Donald Bergus, a foreign service officer, complicated matters by offering to help the Egyptian government compose a draft of its position more acceptable to the United States. The draft was leaked to the press by the Egyptian foreign minister as an "acceptable" American position; it was promptly disavowed by Washington, leading to charges of perfidy by both Egypt and Israel. See Joseph Kraft, "Phantom memorandum," Washington Post (June 27, 1971). Also see Anwar es-Sadat, "We are now back to square one," Newsweek (December 13, 1971), pp. 43-44, 47, and Golda Meir, "Address to Knesset," Jerusalem Post (weekly overseas ed., October 7, 1971).

31. William P. Rogers, "A legacy for peace: our responsibility to further generations," address to the UN General Assembly on October 4, 1971, Depart. of State Bull. (October 25, 1971), pp. 442-444. Israeli Premier Golda Meir criticized the speech vigorously as an example of American "backsliding" from what she had been told in June.

32. See Robert J. Pranger, American Policy for Peace in the Middle

East, 1969-1971: Problems of Principle, Maneuver and Time. Washington: Amer. Enterprise Instit. for Public Policy Research (December 1971).

33. Kalb and Kalb, p. 209.

34. U.S. Foreign Policy for the 1970's: The Emerging Structure of Peace, a report to the Congress by President Richard Nixon. Washington: GPO (February 9, 1972), p. 149.

35. Tad Szulc, "Behind the Vietnam cease-fire agreement," Foreign Policy (Summer 1974), p. 41.

36. U.S. Foreign Policy for the 1970's . . . , p. 140.

37. One version of KGB influence in Egypt appears in chapter 2 of John Barron, KGB: The Secret Work of Soviet Secret Agents. New York: Dutton (1974).

38. The Sudanese Communist Party, fearing correctly an imminent purge by General Ja'far Numayry's government in the context of Sudanese accession to the new Federation, launched a sudden coup and arrested the general. Both Sadat and Numayry could not fail to have been impressed with the stalling tactics of Soviet advisers at Wadd Saidna base, where the Sudanese brigade assigned to the defense of the Suez Canal was attempting to effect a rescue. After his successful restoration, Numayry expelled the Soviet advisory mission. See Peter K. Bechtold, "Military rule in the Sudan: the first five years of Ja'far Numayry," Middle East J. (Winter 1975), pp. 23-26.

39. Anwar es-Sadat, "Broadcast to the nation," Voice of the Arabs Radio on January 13, 1972, New Middle East (February 1972), p. 42. See also the Sadat interviews in Newsweek (December 13, 1971, and March 6, 1972).

40. See "Will the Russians change their ways?" U.S. News & World Report (June 12, 1972), p. 18.

41. War Minister Sadek, having demonstrated his ability to present army grievances, became too powerful for Sadat's liking, especially in view of the late Marshal Hakim Amer's precedent; he was removed several months later amid rumors of an impending coup. For an account of the Amer-Nasser relationship, see Robert Stephens, Nasser: A Political Biography. New York: Simon & Schuster (1971), pp. 359-362.

42. Whetten, pp. 223-224.

43. This activity soon cost Sadat the support of Colonel Qadaffi. A series of quixotic exchanges between the two over Egyptian foreign policy and the progress of the new Federation led to a mass Libyan march on Cairo to effect the union by brotherly love. This crusade was halted near El Alamein when the Egyptians blocked the highway with railway coaches. Sadat received a delegation and accepted a petition signed in blood; the marchers then dispersed. This incident and the Libyan plane disaster in February 1973 opened an irreparable breach that has been widened further by vituperative personal exchanges, such as Libyan charges that Sadat was

corrupt and Sadat's reply that Qadaffi was "one hundred percent sick and possessed by the devil."

44. Joel Darmstadter and Hans H. Landsberg, "The economic background," Daedalus (Fall 1975), pp. 22-25.

45. The full story of the Libyan revolution has yet to be told. According to one version, the Senussi King Idris, who was traveling abroad when the coup occurred, informed the United States and the United Kingdom that this was *his* coup against the troublesome crown prince. Colonel (then Lieutenant) Qadaffi surprised everyone since he was an unknown figure. See Ruth First, Libya: The Elusive Revolution. New York: Africana (1975), pp. 100-115.

46. Edith Penrose, "The development of crisis," Daedalus (Fall 1975), pp. 41-42. Algeria and Iraq also used the confiscation technique to play the companies against one another.

47. Ibid., p. 48. The participation agreements, which gave the governments a share of produced oil to "sell" on the open market, also presumed market prices lower than the posted prices.

48. James E. Akins, "The oil crisis: this time the wolf is here," in William P. Bundy [ed.], The World Economic Crisis. New York: Norton (1975), pp. 21-22. The article was published originally in Foreign Affairs (July 1973).

49. Ibid. See also Stephen G. Breyer and Paul W. MacAvoy, Energy Regulation by the Federal Power Commission. Washington: Brookings Instit. (1974), pp. 56-88, 122.

50. Penrose, pp. 45-49. See also Petroleum Intelligence Weekly (August 14, 1972; November 6, 1972; December 25, 1972).

51. See Foy D. Kohler, Leon Gouré and Mose L. Harvey, The Soviet Union and the October 1973 Middle East War: The Implications for Détente. Miami: Univ. of Miami Center for Advanced Internatl. Studies, Monograph in Internatl. Affairs (1974), p. 37.

52. Ibid., p. 39; Whetten, p. 234.

53. Lester A. Sobel [ed.], Israel and the Arabs: The October 1973 War. New York: Facts on File (1974), p. 58.

54. Kohler, Gouré and Harvey, pp. 39-41.

55. "General Ismail and the war," excerpts from an interview conducted by Muhammad Hassanain Heikal on November 18, 1973, J. of Palestine Studies (Winter 1974), pp. 216-217 et passim.

56. C.L. Sulzberger, Postscript with a Chinese Accent. New York: Macmillan (1974), p. 26.

57. For example, see FBIS (September 6-8, 1972) after the Munich massacre.

58. Interviews conducted by the author and Dr. William R. Kintner with various Israeli diplomats during May 1973.

59. See the Jerusalem Post (weekly overseas ed., June 12, 1973).

60. See Gitelson.

61. U.S. Foreign Policy for the 1970's: Shaping a Durable Peace, a report to the Congress by President Richard Nixon. Washington: GPO (May 3, 1973), p. 13.

62. U.S. Senate, Committee on Foreign Relations, Subcommittee on Multinational Corporations, 93rd Congress, 2nd Sess.; Hearings, Multinational Petroleum Companies and Foreign Policy. Washington: GPO (June 20, 1974), p. 515.

63. Ibid., p. 504.

64. Agranat Investigating Committee, The Yom Kippur War: Partial Report [in Hebrew], hereafter cited as the Agranat Report. Jerusalem, n.p. (1974), p. 29.

65. New York Times (July 26, 1972).

66. New York Times (June 23, 1973).

67. "Using U.S. military strength as an instrument for peace," excerpts of remarks by President Nixon, Depart. of State Bull. (June 11, 1973), p. 839.

68. Sulzberger, p. 241.

69. "Encouraging a negotiating process in the Middle East," address by Joseph J. Sisco, Assistant Secretary of State for Near Eastern and South Asian Affairs, Depart. of State Bull. (June 11, 1973), pp. 847-848.

70. Sulzberger, pp. 240-241.

71. "Furthering peace in the Middle East," toast by Secretary Kissinger on September 29, 1975, at a dinner at the U.S. Mission to the UN in honor of the Arab League delegations to the UN, Depart. of State Bull. (October 20, 1975), p. 58.

72. The primary source for the early events of the war from the Israeli point of view is the Agranat Report.

73. The Day of Atonement is a major Jewish holy day, marked by prayer, fasting and the blowing of the Ram's Horn. The month of Ramadan is observed by Muslims with special prayers and fasting during the daylight hours, followed by feasting after nightfall. In 1973, 10 Ramadan was the 1,350th anniversary of the Battle of Badr, which had facilitated Mohammed's capture of Mecca. Hence the Egyptian code name Operation Badr.

74. Foreign Minister Abba Eban, quoted in Daniel Gottlieb, "U.N. meeting," Jerusalem Post (weekly overseas ed., October 9, 1973); author's interview with a member of Israeli intelligence in May 1974; see also Kalb and Kalb, p. 457.

75. The Agranat Report mentions this concern without comment; neither Mrs. Meir nor Moshe Dayan has introduced American "warnings" against pre-emption as a defense for their actions. The Kalbs' account (p. 459), which apparently relied heavily on Kissinger's own recollections, mentions the secretary of state's warning against pre-emption.

76. Jobert asked why "trying to set foot on one's own territory

necessarily constituted an unexpected aggression." See the New York Times (October 9, 1973).

77. Kalb and Kalb, p. 459.

78. Chaim Herzog, The Yom Kippur War [in Hebrew]. Jerusalem: Edanim (1975), p. 20.

79. See the Agranat Report; Jerusalem Post (weekly overseas ed., October 21 and 28, 1975); and Martin van Creveld, Military Lessons of the Yom Kippur War: Historical Perspectives. Beverly Hills: Sage, Washington Paper No. 24 (1975), p. 13.

80. See General Henry A. Miley, Jr., "Lessons Learned: Mid-East war logistics," Army Logistician (July/August 1974), pp. 3-4. General Miley described the Israeli logistical problem succinctly: "Under the conditions I described earlier—no pipeline and virtually no production base—a lengthy war effort cannot be sustained. The 21-day war in October was 14 days too long."

81. See, for instance, Joseph Kraft, "Letter from Israel," New Yorker (February 11, 1974), pp. 102-111, and Amos Perlmutter, "The covenant of war," Harper's Magazine (February 1974), pp. 51-61.

82. New York Times (October 9, 1973).

83. Jerusalem Post (weekly overseas ed., October 16, 1973).

84. Walter Laqueur, Confrontation: The Middle East and World Politics. New York: Quadrangle (1974), pp. 100-101, 110.

85. Kalb and Kalb, p. 456.

86. Robert Hotz, "The Mideast surprise," Aviation Week & Space Tech. (October 15, 1974), p. 7; also see "Soviet aid sparks Arab gains," ibid., p. 12.

87. New York Times (October 9, 1973) and Washington Star News, quoted in Jerusalem Post (weekly overseas ed., October 16, 1973).

88. See the statement made by U.S. Representative to the United Nations John Scali on October 8, 1973, Depart. of State Bull. (November 12, 1973), pp. 598-599.

89. The Kalbs' account is contested substantially by Tad Szulc, "Is he indispensable? answers to the Kissinger riddle," New York Magazine (July 1, 1974) and by Edward Luttwak and Walter Laqueur, "Kissinger and the Yom Kippur war," Commentary (September 1974).

90. William B. Quandt, "Kissinger and the Arab-Israeli disengagement negotiations," J. of Internatl. Affairs (November 1, 1975), pp. 36-37.

91. "Dayan on U.S. aid," excerpts from interview on October 20, 1973, Aviation Week & Space Tech. (October 29, 1973), p. 7. Kissinger later claimed that Israel would have collapsed for lack of ammunition without the U.S. airlift. New York Times (November 24, 1975).

92. Henry Kissinger, "Moral purposes and policy choices," address before the Third Pacem in Terris Conference, Washington, D.C., on October 8, 1973, Depart. of State Bull. (October 29, 1973), p. 528.

93. Ibid., p. 529.

94. These exhortations produced results. According to President Sadat, President Boumédienne of Algeria, to whom the Soviet message was originally delivered, spent $200 million for weapons shipped to Egypt and Syria during the war. "Speech by Egyptian President Anwar es-Sadat at May Day ceremony in Asyut—live," Cairo Domestic Service in Arabic, on May 1, 1975, FBIS (May 2, 1975), p. D10.

95. "Secretary Kissinger's news conference of October 12," Depart. of State Bull. (October 29, 1973), p. 535.

96. Ibid., p. 537.

97. Ibid., p. 538.

98. "As Sadat addresses Arab Socialist Union Secretariat General," Cairo Domestic Service in Arabic, on September 15, 1975, FBIS (September 16, 1975), p. D5; also see Quandt, p. 38.

99. "As Sadat addresses . . . , pp. D5-D6.

100. Kalb and Kalb, p. 471.

101. Federal Energy Office, Hearings Before the Permanent Subcommittee on Investigations, U.S. Senate, 93rd Congress, 1st Sess., part 5. Washington: GPO (January 25, 1974), p. 606-609.

102. "Text of the resolution of OAPEC, 17 October 1973," Times, London (November 17, 1973).

103. Szulc, p. 33.

104. Leslie H. Gelb, "House ends study of October alert," New York Times (April 10, 1974). The letter, typewritten in English, supposedly contained four paragraphs, the third of which stated that if the United States would not join the Soviet Union in enforcing the cease-fire, "we should be faced with the necessity urgently to consider the question of taking appropriate steps unilaterally." It closed with Brezhnev's reiteration that he valued the Soviet-American "relationship."

105. Defcon-3, or Defense Condition 3, was a precautionary stage that did not place American armed forces on a war footing. Leaves were canceled, fifty to sixty B-52s returned from Guam to the United States, and another U.S. attack aircraft carrier was ordered to join the two already "on station" in the Mediterranean with the Sixth Fleet. The general Defcon-3 lasted until October 31, when the Soviet airlift resumed its previous pattern and Israel agreed to permit resupply of the Third Army.

106. Elmo R. Zumwalt, Jr., and Worth Bagley, "What détente means to the USSR," part 1 of Détente. New York: Special Features, a syndicated service of the New York Times (September 11, 1975), p. 4. Zumwalt described the Brezhnev letter as "savage" and added: "It reminded me of notes we sent the Soviets during the Cuban missile crisis, when we felt the security of the U.S. was at stake." The admiral also said that Soviet naval vessels outnumbered the American Sixth Fleet by three to two and could bring to bear overwhelming air power from friendly airfields in the Arab states and Yugoslavia. See "Soviet threat to U.S. prevented Israel's destruction of 3rd Army," Jerusalem Post (weekly overseas ed., August 5, 1975). Also see Zumwalt's address "Implications of the decline of American

power," American Zionist (November, 1975). For a good discussion of U.S.-Soviet forces in the Mediterranean, see Whetten, "Has parity been achieved?" (appendix B).

107. Kalb and Kalb, p. 484.

108. "Secretary Kissinger's news conference on October 25," Depart. of State Bull. (November 12, 1973), p. 589.

109. Ibid., p. 592. Secretary of Defense Schlesinger confirmed this the next day. See "Secretary of Defense Schlesinger's news conference of October 26," Depart. of State Bull. (November 19, 1973), pp. 620-621.

110. "Secretary Kissinger's news conference on October 25," pp. 590, 592.

111. Ibid., p. 591.

112. "President Nixon's news conference of October 26," Depart. of State Bull. (November 12, 1973), p. 583.

113. Ibid.

114. "Secretary Kissinger's news conference on October 25," p. 587.

115. Josef Harif, "The ultimatum of Kissinger" [in Hebrew], Ma'ariv, Tel Aviv (November 2, 1973). A spirited debate has emerged over whether the U.S. threatened her own intervention to save the Third Army. See letters to the editor, Commentary (September 1975), pp. 20-24.

116. From the Knesset debate on the Israeli prisoners of war issue; quoted in Harif.

117. "President Nixon's news conference of October 26," p. 584; "Secretary of Defense Schlesinger's news conference of October 26," pp. 625-626; New York Times (October 26, 1973).

118. New York Times (October 31, 1973).

119. Many of these originated in the debate over Kissinger's Middle East policies. See, for example, Eugene V. Rostow, "America, Europe and the Middle East," Commentary (February 1974) and Theodore Draper, "Détente," Commentary (June 1974).

120. "How to pass peacefully the seven lean years" [in Hebrew], conversation with the prime minister conducted by Joel Marcus, Ma'ariv (December 3, 1974). An English version appears in FBIS (December 4, 1974), p. N1. The interview proved controversial in Israel and abroad. See the editorial entitled "Rearguard battle" in the usually pro-government Jerusalem Post (weekly overseas ed., December 9, 1974).

121. See Wolfgång Hager, "A new challenge to the European Community," in Curt Gasteyger [ed.], The Western World and Energy. Paris: The Atlantic Instit. for Internatl. Affairs, Atlantic Paper No. 1 (1974), p. 61.

122. John A. Cicco, Jr., "The Atlantic Alliance and the Arab challenge: the European perspective," World Affairs (Spring 1975), p. 304 et passim.

123. U.S. Oil Companies and the Arab Oil Embargo: The International Allocation of Constricted Supplies, prepared by the Federal Energy Admin.'s Office of Internatl. Energy Affairs for the Subcommittee on

Multinatl. Corporations of the Committee on Foreign Relations, U.S. Senate. Washington: GPO (1975), p. 4. The companies were not very successful, in part because of their abrupt enforcement in early November of a secondary boycott on petroleum products supplied to the U.S. military. See U.S. Senate, Committee on Government Operations, Permanent Subcommittee on Investigations, 93rd Congress, 2nd Sess.; Hearings, Current Energy Shortages Oversight Series, Cutoff of Petroleum Products to U.S. Military Forces, part 8. Washington: GPO (April 22, 1974). Their actions were also severely resented in Japan and apparently played a large part in the Tanaka government's decision to endorse the Arab position on November 22, "the first open break with American foreign policy in post-war diplomatic history that Japan had dared to make." See Yoshi Tsurumi, "Japan," Daedalus (Fall 1975), pp. 123-124.

124. "U.S. Oil Companies and the Arab Oil Embargo . . . ," p. 9.

125. Ibid., p. 5.

126. See Romano Prodi and Alberto Clo, "Europe," Daedalus (Fall 1975). The Japanese, even more dependent on Middle East oil than Europe, also experienced no shortage, but the Tanaka government equaled the West Europeans in its ignorance and panic. Tsurumi, pp. 119, 123-124.

127. Petroleum Economist (February 1974), p. 48; Petroleum Economist (May 1974), p. 165. The effect on individual state revenues was electrifying: Saudi Arabia's earnings, less than $1 billion in 1965 and approximately $2 billion in 1970, would now be close to $5 billion for 1973.

128. For Kissinger's maiden effort on these unfamiliar subjects, see "Kissinger on oil, food and trade," Business Week (January 13, 1975).

129. The nine EC states, Canada, Japan and Norway were the original invitees; they were joined later by EC and OECD representatives.

130. New York Times (February 6, 1974).

131. "Interdependence and cooperative solutions," speech by Henry A. Kissinger, U.S. secretary of state, delivered at the Washington Energy Conference, Washington, D.C., on February 11, 1974, Vital Speeches (March 15, 1974), p. 3,254. He predicted a current account payments deficit of more than $36 billion for the industrial states and a $25- to $30-billion deficit for the less developed countries—thrice the foreign aid flow of the past year.

132. One analyst estimated that OPEC's oil market could not be reduced below 25 million barrels per day before the early 1980s, a full 10 to 12 million barrels daily below OPEC's capacity. By pro-rating production, principally in Saudi Arabia and Kuwait, OPEC might manage this reduction without seriously interfering with plans for local development. Thomas O. Enders, "OPEC and the industrial countries: the next ten years," Foreign Affairs (July 1975).

133. International Economic Report of the President, Together with the Annual Report of the Council on Internatl. Economic Policy; trans-